GOOD FOOD IN MEXICO CITY

A GUIDE TO FOOD STALLS, FONDAS AND FINE DINING

BY

NICHOLAS GILMAN

iUniverse, Inc.
New York   Bloomington

Good Food in Mexico City
A Guide to Food Stalls, Fondas and Fine Dining

iUniverse books may be ordered through booksellers or by contacting:

iUniverse
1663 Liberty Drive
Bloomington, IN 47403
www.iuniverse.com
1-800-Authors (1-800-288-4677)

ISBN: 978-1-60528-027-1 (pbk)
ISBN: 978-0-595-63158-2 (ebk)

Printed in the United States of America

Cover Design: Nicholas Gilman
Cover Photo: Luz Montero

Acknowledgements

For Lynn Nesbit, the first person in my life to introduce me to the pleasures of fine food;

For Kathy Erteman my "partner in crime" in the quest for the authentic;

For Stan Gray and Bill Reiner, our frequent dining partners and lovers of great cooking;

And, finally, to Jim Johnston, without whose loving patience this book would not exist.

I also want to thank the following for their invaluable help in producing this book:

Valeria Clark, Carol Romano, Leticia Alexander, Regina Gomez & Angel Valtierra, Ruth Alegría, Tom Friedman, David Lida, Suzanne Kimball, Luis and Elodie Santamaria,Veronica Moctezuma Rivera, Pedro Gellert, Eugenia Meyer, Meredith Brody, Rachel Laudan, Lynette Seator, Michael Parker, Daniel Barrón, Aran & Margot Shetterly, Ceci Connoly, Luz Montero

And last but not least, to my high school teachers Miss Mayer (Connie Boyers) and the late great Miss T for trying to teach me how to write good I mean well.

CONTENTS

MACHO MOUTH
By David Lida

Mexico City is a perpetual picnic. Literally: There is a dizzying amount of wonderful food here, and the majority of it is consumed standing on one's feet, on the scarred and broken concrete sidewalk. It is dispensed from whitewashed metal stands, doled out of baskets and buckets, fried on griddles barely balanced over planks, ladled out of huge metal pots.

When I came to live here in 1990, I suffered from the foreigner's mistrustful hypersensitivy to the hazards of bacterias and amoebas. Transcendentally alert to anything that passed my lips, a dog soldier engaged in germ warfare, nothing was above suspicion. Could I trust that lettuce leaf wilting unapologetically on the edge of the plate? The puddle of orange grease surrounding the cochinita tacos? Did I dare to swallow some chopped squiggle of meat whose name I didn't even know?

I soon began to drop my guard, sampling raw ceviche in markets, the darkest depths of a pig's innards in tacos filled with carnitas, quesadillas stuffed with sautéed brains. There was rarely any intestinal consequence, and the results were so delicious that I became a dedicated culinary adventurer, a macho where my mouth was concerned.

If the glories of Mexico City can be consumed inexpensively every day on its sidewalks, it is important to appreciate that the combined textures, colors and flavors of Mexican cuisine make it the most sophisticated and subtle of the American continent. The biggest city in the Western hemisphere, of course, has its share of exquisite and important white-table cloth restaurants. They cater not just to people who are playing it safe, but to those who can appreciate – and afford – their superb offerings.

Finding out where and what to eat in any big city is a puzzle: thorny, enigmatic, potentially frustrating and disappointing. It is marvelous to finally build the experience to solve that mystery. The book you have in your hands will save you years of effort. Within its pages are the secrets to eating in Mexico City.

David Lida is the author of *First Stop in the New World: Mexico City, Capital of the 21st Century* (Riverhead Books).

INTRODUCTION

Like many world cuisines, the food of Mexico has poor representation outside of its homeland. But in the country itself, one can sample a huge variety of regional variations made from ingredients and techniques only found here. Mexico City is the center of power and culture from which everything in the republic emanates and it is here that the traditions are collected and studied. In recent years a culinary establishment has developed, headed by chefs, scholars and historians. Cookbooks have been produced, *"alta cocina"* restaurants have opened featuring gussied up traditional dishes and in general, there has been a revival of interest amongst the middle and upper classes in classic Mexican food; the working classes never abandoned their customs. At a time of great globalization, locally accelerated by the free trade agreements of the 1990's, some culinary schools and chefs are teaching methods of food preparation that, while in the past handed down by word of mouth, would in a generation or two, have been all but forgotten. Author Diana Kennedy became the "Julia Child" of Mexico, publishing some of the first seriously researched cookbooks in English, thus legitimizing this hitherto misunderstood branch of Latino culture. We, the curious diners, benefit from all this by the proliferation in the capital of distinctly "Mexican" eateries of every description, from old-fashioned holes-in-the-wall to elegant temples of fusion "cuisine".

Contemporary Mexico City is home to small communities of foreigners as well as a growing number of locals whose sophisticated palettes require tastes beyond local cuisine. Italian, Argentine, French and Japanese restaurants are increaslingly popular. Pseudo-Chinese joints are abundant, but "authentic" Asian food is hard to come by, due to the lack of an immigrant population (except for a small Korean community.) Very good European restaurants have appeared in recent years; before the early nineties, the only French restaurants were of the 1950's American type, serving heavy, uninspired dishes. Nowadays, representatives of France, Spain and Italy rival restaurants from their native countries in quality. Prices tend to be comparatively low making a 3-star meal at such places as Tezka or Le Cirque a relative bargain.

This guide, a fattening labor of love, will help the visitor and resident alike to sort through as many as 36,000 eating establishments. While by no means all-encompassing, we have chosen to concentrate on neighborhoods more likely to be frequented by visitors. The information in the book has been culled from the experience of the author as well as from that of friends and acquaintances; assessments are necessarily opinionated and subjective.

People will sometimes disagree with our judgments, and will have other experiences, bad or good. Kitchens vary, quality goes up and down, there are successful and disastrous days. No place, (not even Tour D'Argent in Paris) is completely predictable or dependable. So use this book as a guide, not as gospel.

Nicholas Gilman
Mexico City

THE HISTORY OF MEXICAN FOOD

The history of Mexican "cuisine" as such goes back to the cultivation of the first corn plants, more than 6000 years ago. The lowly but revered tortilla has not changed in any way shape or form since around 600 AD when remains of the earliest *comales* are found and, in fact, it is the one true pre-Hispanic food still eaten today. Many forms of maize consumption resemble those developed hundreds or thousands of years ago: the tamal (the singular word for tamales) and the taco immediately come to mind. But outside influences have affected the way things are done and steered the natural development and growth of this great *mestizo* culture. With the conquest, the Spaniards brought plants and animals to the continent that no one knew, such as cattle, pigs, sheep, goats, and chickens. Among the plants and condiments introduced were olive oil, spices such as cinnamon, parsley, coriander, oregano and ginger. nuts and grains such as almonds, rice, wheat, and barley; fruit and vegetables such as apples, oranges, grapes, lettuce, carrots, cauliflowers, eggplant, potatoes, (brought from Peru), and sugarcane. From the galleons of Manila came such exotic Asian foods as mangos, tamarind, cloves, nutmeg, black pepper and vanilla. Tamales are made with pork fat, introduced by the Spanish; tacos with ingredients too varied to enumerate. Cooking techniques such as stewing and frying in oil were not known before the conquest, as the indigenous people used no animal fats in which to cook. Spanish foods and culinary concepts were influenced by the Moors and Sephardic Jews, which left its mark on Mexican cuisine. The Spaniards brought many ingredients back to the old world with them, which had a wide influence; these included tomatoes, chilies, squash, corn, chocolate and pineapples. But few settlers were women: female indigenous cooks, therefore, were employed and they, too, brought their knowledge and traditions to *criollo* kitchens. Although not as many African slaves were brought over as were in other American countries (there were plenty of locals to exploit) there was some influence of these rich cultures, especially along the coasts. Chinese workers came to build the railroads in the 19th century and left their mark, before being subsumed into the general population. There was a wave of German immigration, and of European Jews, as well as Lebanese. and again the Spanish (this time welcome) as exiles from Franco's dictatorship. And of course, more recently, with the supposed opening up of borders, an influx of North American, i.e. fast food "culture" has arrived.

True *Cocina Mexicana*, therefore, is a *mestizaje,* or blend, of many cuisines, but the strongest influence remains that which has its roots in the indestructible native cultures of Mexico itself.

Market scene by Diego Rivera

THE WOMEN OF MEXICAN CUISINE

Since pre-conquest times, women have prepared the food in Mexico; they ground the corn, patted out the tortillas, and prepared the *guisos*, or cooked dishes. They were the ones who incorporated the new ingredients and techniques brought by the Spaniards. As few Spanish women came to the new world in the early years, indigenous women and sometimes African slaves were employed in the conquistador's kitchens. They ruled the larders of the large haciendas and continued to develop a true *mestizo* cuisine.

Knowledge of recipes and techniques were passed down generation to generation until our era. Not until the last decades of the 20th century did young women have options other than to be housekeepers and cooks. Even in recent decades a woman's occupation was often written on official forms as *"labores propias de su sexo"* or "work appropriate to her sex." As women's lives changed, the store of culinary knowledge began to be lost. Information long kept private and not shared outside of the family was no longer valued by those destined to inherit it.

To this day few culinary institutes in Mexico teach techniques of classical Mexican cooking. Since the 1980's, however, many women chefs (notably, Alicia Gironella de Angeli, Patricia Quintana, Monica Patiño, Martha Ortiz Chapa and Carmen Tititia) have opened their own restaurants to international acclaim, with the aim of promoting both traditional and innovative Mexican cuisine.

Before them came women who promoted the culture of Mexican cooking, including Lula Bertrán, María Orsini, María Dolores Yzabal, Janet Long and Lila Lomelí. Most of their work sought to improve restaurant standards, promote Mexican food outside the country, organize food festivals, write books, collect regional recipes. They in turn followed earlier generations of women, among them, Josefina Velázquez de León, Adela Hernández and even artists and arbiters of culture like Frida Kahlo, Olga Costa and Lupe Mariín who celebrated all things Mexican. Outside of Mexico, it was also principally women who spread the word: Diana Kennedy, Josefina Howard, and Zarela Martinez are some of the most notable. Recently, collected knowledge from home and abroad has begun to be taught in a few culinary institutes in Mexico. While we must recognize the accomplishments of male chefs and scholars, such as Rick Bayless, Ricardo Muñoz, Salvador Novo and Jose Iturriaga, in no other world cuisine have women been so recognized and celebrated for their important contributions.

Market Vendors, by Esther Gilman, oil on canvas, 1947

HOW TO USE THIS BOOK

Following an established format, we have rated each establishment with a "$", from one to three: one $ means under US $10, $$, US 10-25, $$$ over US 25. This is per person, including tip and one drink. Street Stalls and Fondas are all in the one "$" category and so do not receive individual ratings. While we have not specifically indicated whether credit cards are accepted, at most places in the "restaurant" category they are, at cantinas, fondas, markets and street stalls they are not. If you are not sure, call and check. Most (but not all) restaurants that take cards still accept American Express in Mexico. Tipping is not expected in low end establishments such as stands; anywhere you sit down, however, a few pesos tip is appropriate. At fancier places, 10-15% is the norm, a little less than in the US; but more will certainly be appreciated in this difficult economy.

Nearby metro stops are indicated; if not, it means there is no metro within 8 blocks.

Larger chapters are divided by Colonia or zone (i.e. Centro, Condesa etc.) and within those categories listings are alphabetical.

The opening year follows listings which are distinguished by their antiquity.

Places not on the maps are indicated as such.

At the end of the book there is a glossary where the reader will find explanations of Spanish words or culinary terminology with which they may be unfamiliar.

Check out our website for updates and additions:
WWW.MEXICOCITYFOOD.NET

Carnitas!

STREET FOOD AND MARKET STALLS

STREET FOOD AND MARKET STALLS

Some of the most delicious and authentic food in Mexico is found in street stalls (*puestos* in Spanish) and markets. It is common advice not to eat ANYTHING on the street; even some Mexicans adhere to this rule. I don't find it necessary to be so strict, as many stands are simply micro-restaurants whose ingredients, facilities and handlers are as spic-and-span as a hospital kitchen. What's more, you can see everything that goes on, which is comforting. It took me several years to work up the courage to start eating food from street stalls because I assumed that all of it was greasy and loaded with bacteria. While there is no guarantee of germ-free food, even in fancy restaurants, I follow some basic guidelines when choosing where to eat.

Check out the stall and the cook for cleanliness. If it doesn't look clean, forget it. I choose food that I can see being cooked, and avoid anything that looks too greasy. I stay away from things cooked in deep fat, unless I can see that the oil is clean and very hot. I don't eat dishes that look like they have been sitting outside for a long time. I look for crowded stalls that have been discovered by locals: they have already selected the good ones. Some vendors slip on a plastic glove before accepting money, a good sign. Make sure your hands are clean before you eat. I carry a package of moist towelettes with me, or a good alternative is the sanitizing drops now available. I avoid certain kinds of street food, such as seafood, during hot weather.

In all but the most unsavory places these days, bottled, purified water is used to make ice and drinks such as *aguas frescas*; ask if you like, but it is not necessary in a fancier establishment. The same goes for the raw vegetable rule, i.e., in middle-level places on up, vegetables will inevitably be disinfected, otherwise ask or avoid. All the places recommended here have been tried and we have never gotten sick. But I can't guarantee you won't; sometimes you just have to keep your fingers crossed and go for it!

In this section we recommend *puestos* found on the street, in covered markets, and in temporary street markets, called "*Tianguis*".

A typical *puesto*

FLAUTAS AND CALDOS

Flautas are something I always avoided, as they looked like scary grease bombs; then I read an article in which well-known Mexican cultural icons name their favorite Mexican dishes. Alternative dramaturge Jesusa Rogriguez was quick to laud these humble snacks as her pick, so I had to try them…and I was hooked. At their best, these elongated tortillas rolled and deep-fried (hence the name "flute"), containing *barbacoa* (pork or mutton), chicken, potatoes or cheese, topped with cream and salsa verde or guacamole and sprinkled with grated *queso fresco* and lettuce are the essential Mexican *antojito*. And for some reason, they are often served alongside *caldo de gallina*, that is, the best chicken soup your mother never made.

Caldos de Gallina/Flautas Chilpancingo
Calle Chilpancingo, the fourth stand from the corner of Av. Nuevo León, Condesa
Metro or Metrobus Chilpancingo
Open Monday through Friday 11-5pm

This stand on Chilpancingo is one of the best and is packed at comida-time, 2-4pm. You can have your soup with *pechuga* (breast), *muslo* (thigh) or no extra meat at all, and flautas are sold by the piece.

Other, similar places to try flautas or caldos are:

El Gallinazo, serving only caldos, located on Puente de Alvarado, south side in front of the "Viana" near the metro Revolución exit, Colonia Santa Maria la Ribera. (not on map)

Tianguis Condesa on Tuesdays only, on calle Agustín Melgar, near Pachuca, are several caldos and flautas tables, across from the fresh fish stand. Open approximately 9-4pm

Mercado La Merced - Caldos de Gallina "Vale"
Along the west side of the main building, exiting by *puerta* 25 or 26.
Tianguis Roma, Wednesdays, Calle el Oro, near Insurgentes, Metro Insurgentes

Also see: El Paisa (p. 43)
                  Tio Pedro (p.50)

FISH AND SEAFOOD

El Caguamo
Calle Ayuntamento, corner of Lopez, Centro
Metro Salto de Agua
Open Monday through Saturday, 11-6pm

The name is slang for a liter size beer bottle, but it is seafood they serve here. This well known *puesto de mariscos* is always full of returning customers, indicating fresh and sanitary merchandise. The ceviches of either *jaiba, pescado, calamar* or *pulpo*, made with chopped tomato, chile, onion and cilantro and augmented with lime and olive oil are out this world, and can be eaten as a *coctél*, in a glass, or on a tostada. The *caldo de camarón* is a rich, deep, red broth flavored with dried and fresh shrimp and chillies; a *"chico"*, served in a cup, usually does it for me. *Filetes*, boned fish filets battered and deep fried should be hot: make sure to order one if you see them come fresh out of the oil. Also good are the *empanadas de camarón*, made from fresh rolled dough, but I like to request *"sin mayonesa"*; it's not that I'm Kosher but mayo and seafood is anathema to me. This is a must-stop for aficionados of the real thing...

Ostionería La Morenita
Inside the Mercado Medellín, Between Medellín and Monterrey, Campeche and Coahuila, Roma
Metro Chilpancingo
Open daily until around 5pm.

The tranquil Mercado Medellín in the heart of colonia Roma, is well known for its fresh, high quality produce and sometimes unusual merchandise: several stands offer products from Colombia, Argentina and Cuba, as well as from the Yucatán. The regular *comedores* are popular, but especially beloved are the *marisquerías*. Best of the lot is La Morenita. Gorging on a bowl of *Sopa Especial de Mariscos*, a rich fish broth enlivened with a mix of more kinds of seafood than one can discern, and a plate of *quesadillas de cazón*, surrounded by the sights and sounds of the bustling market, is my idea of a good time. Also tasty is the *Mojarra al mojo de Ajo,* a whole fish fried with lots of garlic. Fruit juices or *aguas preparadas* can be ordered from the stand next door.

Similar fare is also available at:

Mercado San Pedro de los Pinos, in the Colonia of the same name, 3 blocks east of the metro exit. (not on map)
Metro: San Pedro de los Pinos
This market is well-known for its seafood and even offers live music at comida time! All the stalls here serve good food, some even provide menus. Try the *mojarra al mojo de ajo.*

Mercado Coyoacán
Located 3 blocks from the center of Coyoacán,
this market is known for its outstanding seafood.
The long, outdoor communal tables of **El Jardín del Pulpo,** at the corner of Malintzin and Ignacio Allende is famous for

its *cocteles de camarón* or *pulpo*.
Open daily Noon-6pm

Tianguis Condesa
Agustin Melgar, between Pachuca and Mazatlan, Condesa
next to the quesadilla stands; good empanadas and *tostadas de ceviche*.
Tuesdays only

Tianguis Condesa
Corner of Nuevo León & Ometusco, Condesa
Right at one end of the market is a table offering a rich *sopa de mariscos,* among other delights from the sea.
Fridays 10am-4pm

Tianguis Cuauhtémoc, Calle Colima and Alvaro Obregón, Roma
Sundays Noon-6pm
Look for Pescaditos "Cha Cha Cha" on Colima.
This table, decorated with sprigs of parsley, has good quesadillas de pescado and tostadas de camarón. The family-run operation provides clean, fresh, home-style food and free compliments for all the ladies.

see Marisqueria Palmas, p.43
La Ostra, p. 61
Contramar, p. 60
Canto de las Sirenas, p.69
La Veracruzana, 46

POZOLE

Pozole is a thick satisfying soup, almost a stew. While there are regional variations all over Mexico, red pozole from Jalisco is the most common, and has a pork and chile base, containing large corn kernels (hominy) and is served with radish, lettuce, onion, oregano and tostadas which you add according to taste.

Pozole Doña Yoli calle San Ildefonso 42,
(upstairs in the commercial plaza) Centro
Metro: Zócalo
Open Monday - Saturday, 12-6pm

This institution must have been written up in some French guidebook, as I often see tourists lapping up the luscious red pozole. The rich broth contains pork, maize, all the trimmings described above, and good tostadas are served on the side, all for 35 pesos. It's a great stop before or after a visit to the wonderful Museo de San Ildefonso next door.

Other good places for pozole are:

Doña Manuela, across from La Catalana (p. 122)
in the **Mercado San Juan**; only on Saturdays.

Tianguis Cuauhtémoc, Wednesdays & Sundays
Calle Colima and Alvaro Obregón

Mercado de Antojitos, Coyoacán, (p. 28)

Mercado San Juan de los Arcos de Belén (p. 122)

For pozole served in restaurants also see:
Pozolería La Casa de Toño (p. 64)
Pozolería Tizka (p. 62)

QUESADILLAS, TLACOYOS AND SOPES

These *antojitos* or snacks are all variations on a theme: *masa* (corn dough) stuffed or topped with prepared fillings. *Quesadillas* are either tortillas, or slabs of fresh masa, filled and cooked on a griddle or in oil. *Tlacoyos* are hand-made eye-shaped dough patties, filled with either fava beans, *frijoles*, or *requeson* cheese, dry-cooked and topped with nopales, cheese and salsa. *Sopes* are thick tortillas, spread with beans, topped with meat and cheese or a prepared filling, salsa and cream.

CENTRO:

Quesadillas Lagunilla
La Lagunilla flea market corner of González Bocanegra and Comonfort, one block from Reforma (not on map)
Metro: Garibaldi
Open Sunday 10am-5pm

Smack in the middle of the antiques section of the flea market is this busy stand specializing in quesadillas as well as sopes and tlacoyos. A successful family-run business that uses fresh ingredients, it serves both shoppers and knowledgeable vendors. We like to order a combo of *espinacas y hong*os or *flor de calabaza y queso* or simply a *"tlacoyo con todo."*

The **Mercado Merced** is the largest public market in the city (aside from the Central de Abastos, the wholesale market.) It is an area stretching for many city blocks, each specializing in its own product. Functioning like the old Les Halles in Paris, the Merced sells to individuals as well as to stores. The original buildings were built in the 1890's; they were replaced in the 1950's. It is easy to reach by metro: Take Line 1 to the "Merced" stop and exit from the front of the train and you will be in the main market building. You can smell the chilies in the metro station!

In a recent *telenovela* (soap opera) a mean, wealthy matriarchal character insults her working class daughter-in-law whom she despises by calling her a "*quesadillera de la Merced,*" or quesadilla maker from the Merced, a moniker I personally would take as a compliment!

COYOACAN:

Mercado de Antojitos
Higuera 6, Coyoacán
Open daily until Midnight or later

This well known garage-like space, a block from Coyoacán's central Plaza, is open late and most people stop here for a rich pozole or the deep-fried quesadillas, which are delicious despite the grease. The *flor de calabaza*, huitlacoche or *sesos* (brains) are particularly good. Funky and full of old-time atmosphere, this place is worth fighting the crowds for. You'd be hard-pressed to find a more authentic array of snacks.

Other Tlacoyo and Quesadilla stands are:

- in front of the **Museo de la Estampa**
  (near the Museo Franz Mayer), Centro

- in the **Condesa Tuesday & Friday Tianguis** (p.23,25)

- outside of the **Mercado Medellín**
  on the Monterrey side, (p. 24)

- outside the **Mercado Coyoacán** (p.24)

- on **calle Chilpancingo**
  near Baja California, Condesa.

TACOS

Tacos are simply filled tortillas. The two basic types are *tacos de guisados*, tacos with prepared fillings, and *tacos de carne*, filled with meat and which include *carnitas* (chopped roast pork), *barbacoa* (pit-roasted sheep or goat), *birria* (spicy goat or mutton stew), *chuleta* (pork) and the celebrated *tacos al pastor* (roasted meat). We list them here by category.

TACOS DE GUISADOS
CENTRO:

Mi Taco Yucateco
Aranda 36 (near Ayuntamiento), around the
corner from the Mercado San Juan, Centro
Metro: Salto de Agua
Open 2:30pm – 6pm (hours vary)

This is a Yucatecan fonda formerly in a rolling pushcart, now installed in a funky hole in the wall. The *cochinita pibil* is savory if a bit greasy; the *pan de cazón* (frijoles, tortilla, fish and salsa) is surprisingly delicate and the *horchata* (a rice drink) is icy and refreshing.
See also:
Tacos de Bacalao, La Lagunilla, (p.35)

CONDESA:

Calle Tlaxcala, (directly across the street from number 159) Condesa
Monday - Friday 10am until they run out of food!

This small red and white striped stand near "the Chilpancingo food row" (see p. 22) is exceptional. The surprise: the mini *chiles en nogada* with the chilies magically stripped of most of their heat and served either as a taco with rice or alone on a plate. Also good is mole with shredded chicken and the chicken or vegetable tortas. The salsas are varied and unusual: somewhat sweet *chipotles en adobo* are always on hand, as is good guacamole. Several plastic seats are available but most people stand.

Several other good *guisados* stands are located around the corner on **Chilpancingo.**

See also:
Tacos El Guero (p. 47)
El Jarocho (p.47)

COYOACAN:

Super Tacos Chupa Cabras
Av. Coyoacán and Universidad, under the highway across from the Sanborn's, Coyoacán
Metro: Coyoacán
Open daily 7am -3am

This stand, near the metro exit, is extremely popular with students and moviegoers from the nearby Cineteca Nacional. The special "Chupa Cabra tacos," a mixture of chorizo and carnitas, are large and filling. Add the salsas, nopales, fried onions and beans as garnishes and you can make a stop here into a one-dish meal, all for 8 pesos.

See also:
El Jarocho (p. 47)
Salon Corona (p.109)

TACOS AL PASTOR

Tacos al pastor is an Arab-influenced dish that appeared only in the 1950's. Roasted meat on a revolving skewer is sliced and served as an open taco, often with a sliver of pineapple and a selection of salsas. A specialty of Mexico City, these are available everywhere, but avoid unknown venues because often the uncooked meat sits out in the open. Recommended are:

La Lechuza
Miguel Angel Quevedo 34 at Insurgentes,
Coyoacán
My friend Rachel and her kids Gabriel and Julia claim these are the best tacos al pastor in the city - and their opinion is well-backed up.

Taquería El Guero
Rio Lerma 59, near Rio Rhin
Colonia Cuauhtémoc
Open 24 hours
This little hole-in-the-wall with 3 or 4 stools serves delicious tacos al pastor as well as barbacoa made of beef (which is unusual). Also unusual is that they never close, not even for Christmas!

See also:
Tacos al pastor "El Huequito" (p.43)
El Tizoncito (p.60)
El Borrego Viudo (p.50)

BIRRIA

Birria, a common street food that originated in the state of Jalisco, is lamb or goat cooked in broth with chili. It is served as tacos with a bowl of broth as accompaniment. Recommended are:

Los Tres Hermanos, Calle Chilpancingo, (between Baja California and Tlaxcala,) Condesa
Monday-Saturday 10am-6pm
This is one of the stands on "Chilpancingo food row"

See also:
Taquería Tlaquepaque (p.44)
La Polar (p.68)

CARNITAS

Carnitas Michoacanas "Don One", Mercado Abelardo L. Rodríguez (off calle del Carmen between Rep. de Venezuela and Rep. de Colombia,) Centro
Metro: Zócalo
Open daily 11am-5pm

Make your way to the oldest surviving indoor market building in the city. Built in the 1930's, the building is worth a visit to see the murals designed by Diego Rivera and executed by artists including Pablo O'Higgins and Isamu Noguchi. They are in a sad state of disrepair, covered by scratched Plexiglas, and one can only hope for a government subsidy to restore them. At the east end of the market is this stand serving juicy, succulent tacos of carnitas with good red or green salsa.
Excellent Carnitas are available at:

Condesa Tuesday Tianguis (p. 23)

Cuauhtémoc Sunday Tianguis (p. 25)

El Rey del Taco, Oscar Wilde 9, Polanco

For more comfortable places to sample carnitas see:
Los Panchos, (p.64)
El Bajio, (p.74)

MIXIOTES

Mixiotes are made of meat, usually lamb or goat but sometimes chicken, seasoned with spices such as cumin, clove and chili and wrapped in a leaf (traditionally a huge maguey cactus paddle) or parchment paper and cooked. They are served as a main dish or as individual tacos.

*Mixiote*s can be sampled at:

Condesa Tuesday Tianguis (p. 24)

Cuauhtémoc Sunday Tianguis (p. 25)

Roma Wednesday Tianguis (p. 23)

TACOS OF ROAST CHICKEN

A few taco stands and eateries offer chicken, smothered in chili and roasted on a revolving spit. One can order either tacos or a section of the whole bird, served with tortillas, sautéed onions, French fries (often too greasy) and a selection of salsas.

Gilipollos - two branches:
Corner Cinco de Mayo and
Isabel La Católica, Centro

Corner of Sevilla and Londres, Zona Rosa
Both open Monday-Saturday until 9pm

This counter-style *rosticería* offers a quarter chicken with chips, sautéed onions and thick tortillas for under US $2; a hearty lunch doesn't get much cheaper. The name is based on the Spanish slang, not Mexican, and it means "fool" or "dummy," a word that is as silly as it sounds.

Roast chicken tacos are succulent at the stand on Av. Balderas, a few blocks south of Juárez, in front of no. 50 as you exit the Juárez metro station.
The 18 peso quarter chicken makes a good, quick, cheap meal.

TORTAS

Mexico's version of the sandwich was, according to legend, invented by an Italian immigrant at the turn of the 20th century. A soft roll called a *bolillo* is filled with a wide range of ingredients. Popular choices are *milanesa* (pounded and fried meat), *pierna* (roast pork) and *choriqueso* (cheese and sausage), but the variety is endless. Garnishes include tomato, onion, avocado, cheese, lettuce, mayonnaise, and of course, chili jalapeño or chipotle.

Tortas Been
Inside the *pasaje* at República del Salvador 152
Metro: Zócalo or Pino Suarez
Open daily, Noon-6pm

This peculiarly named stand is located inside an odd *pasaje*, or mall, which is also home to several stores selling Arabic foods and folkloric costumes. The *tortas of pierna, pollo* or *pavo ahumado* are worth the 10 minute walk from the Zócalo. Their secret is a "shmeer" of *crema* applied to the *bolillo*, adding extra calories and flavor. Order at the cashier then go to the other side and present your receipt.

At the **Lagunilla flea market** as you enter calle Comonfort from Reforma a stand offers tortas or tacos of bacalao (salt cod) and cochinita pibil. The food is hard to resist, especially when washed down with an *horchata de coco* from the stand next door. Sundays only.

See **Don Polo** (p. 68)

There is a good torta stand in the otherwise dull **Mercado Condesa** at the intersection of Michoacán and Tamaulipas in the Condesa.

Tortas Poblanas, Ayuntamiento 25, (near Mercado San Juan) Centro, is a tiny storefront that serves simple tortas of freshly baked *pierna* or *pavo*.

Also see
La Texcocana (p.45)
El Cuadrilatero (p.45)
La Barraca Valenciana (p. 48)
Don Polo (p.67)

TOSTADAS

A *tostada* is a tortilla, crisp-fried and topped with various concoctions: seafood, ceviche, mole, carnitas, etc., then garnished with lettuce, cream and salsa.

Tostadas Coyoacán
Inside the Mercado de Coyoacán, (p.120)
Open daily, Noon-6 pm

This is the most popular of stands that serve mouth-watering platters of prepared food served on crisp tostadas, and with good reason. Among the offerings are *camarón, pulpo, jaiba, ceviche, barbacoa, mole, carnitas* and *adobo*. Order one at a time; the waiters come around frequently, as do vendors of *aguas and juices*. On Saturday and Sunday afternoons it gets quite crowded. This is one of the city's jewels.

Other good places for *tostadas* are:
Tianguis Condesa, Tuesdays (p. 23) and Fridays (p.25)

JUGOS

You will notice fresh fruit juices lined up in a colorful display at street stalls throughout the city. This is one of the joys of being in Mexico: a glass of fresh juice whenever you want it! *Naranja* (orange), *zanahoria* (carrot), *toronja* (grapefruit) and *betabel* (beet) and, in season, *mandarina* (tangerine) are the most common. Try a *vampiro,* a combination of orange, beet, carrot and sometimes celery juice. (Do not order pure beet juice, however; it should always be mixed with other juices).

There are many juice places in the city; these are a few of my favorite:

Jugos Canadá, Cinco 5 de Mayo 47, (near Palma, 1½ blocks from the Zócalo). This is an indoor *juguería* with seats, offering the most extensive list of juices anywhere.

Other juice stands around town:

Av. Sonora, near the corner of Insurgentes, Condesa

Av. Balderas, 54, at the east entrance to Metro Juárez, Centro

Av. Arcos de Belén, south side, at the entrance to Metro Salto de Agua, Centro

Jugería Maria Cristina (1944)
Pino Suarez 18, Centro

All Tianguises, all Mercados.

FONDAS

FONDAS

The literal definition of a *fonda* is a "tavern, inn or small restaurant." But like the terms bistro and trattoria, the meaning has become blurred. There can be high end fondas like the Fonda del Refugio, an elegant restaurant with white tablecloths, for example. But in this section we are referring to small mom-and-pop joints with just a few tables; *taquerías*, simple restaurants serving mostly tacos; and other such popular, unpretentious eating places. Note that fondas do not generally accept credit cards and most are closed at night. All are in the single "$" category.

CENTRO:

Café la Blanca (1930)
5 de Mayo 40, between Isabel la Católica and Motolinía, Centro
Tel. 5510-9260
Open daily, 7am-11pm

This is not technically a fonda but a cafetería, one of an endangered species, an old-time *café de chino*. In the 19th century, Chinese workers came to build the railroads and some of them continued to make a living by opening "fast food" restaurants, similar to the classic American coffee shop or diner. They serve good coffee, sweet rolls and breakfast around the clock and some still have a few nominally Chinese dishes such as "chao mein." But La Blanca is pure Mexicano with a large menu of classic dishes. The Veracruz-style coffee (hot milk and strong coffee poured from two pitchers simultaneously) is great. I like the old, 1940's atmosphere, the bow-tied waiters at the bar and the fact that you can ask for half-orders of most dishes. There were many places like this in the centro when I arrived in the 1970's but few survive unaltered today. It's a good place for breakfast, and its counter is a comfortable place for single diners.

La Casa del Pavo
Motolinia 40, between Madero & 16 de Septiembre, Centro
Metro: Zócalo, Bellas Artes
Open Monday-Saturday 11am-6:45pm

Like its name implies, this ancient, preserved-in-time place serves nothing but turkey: tortas, tacos, breast on a plate, in soup, and with mole. If you missed Thanksgiving, or just wish for Christmas in July, come here. Our friend Cilla likes to get a couple of *tortas para llevar* to take for the long bus trip up to San Miguel de Allende.

Fonda Mi Lupita (1957)
Buentono 22, near Delicias, Centro
Metro: Salto del Agua
Open Monday-Saturday 1pm-6 pm

Not far from the Mercado San Juan, is this tiny fonda, full of old-time ambiance, and offering only sweet, chocolate-y, mole poblano; it is among the best in the city. Order chicken, either *pechuga* or *pierna* with mole, *enchiladas de mole*, served with the traditional garnish of raw onion rings, sesame seeds and crumbled *queso fresco*, or simply mole with rice and tortillas. They also offer mole to take out.

La Gran Cocina Mi Fonda
López 101, Centro
Metro: Salto del Agua,
Open Monday-Saturday Noon-6pm

This simple but charming fonda serves homecooked Spanish-style food with a Mexican touch. With its turquoise walls, yellow wood tables that you often have to share, and waitresses in uniforms, it is a real hold-over from the centro of the 1940's, and the prices seem unchanged since then as well: a full meal often costs no more than US $5. Although paella is the specialty of the house, I like the roast chicken and the Madrid-style *potaje de lentejas*, a lentil soup flavored with chorizo. I go when I feel like a trip back in time.

El Paisa
Ayuntamiento 44, Centro
Metro Salto de Agua
Tel. 5521 4640

Although there is little ambiance,   the food is well above average and prices are right. The specialty here is *caldo de gallina* (chicken soup served with handmade tortillas) but other fonda items are offered, such as milanesa of beef or chicken, and mole, all served with rice, beans, salad and those great tortillas.

Marisqueria Palmas (1950)
Av. Madero 60, (2nd floor) near Isabel la Católica, Centro
Tel. 5512-0567
Metro: Zócalo
Open Monday-Saturday 11am-7pm

"Since 1950" proclaims the sign; just follow the arrows up the stairs to the second floor and you will find yourself in seafood paradise. A good option in the centro, just steps from the Zócalo, this respite from the hustle of downtown offers the usual options for a *marisquería: ceviches, tostadas, filetes*, fish quesadillas and more elaborate *platos fuertes*, such as aromatic and juicy *camarones al ajillo* (large shrimps sautéed with garlic and slices of guajillo chili). Prices remain low and service is good.

Tacos Al Pastor "El Huequito" (1959)
Ayuntamiento 21, corner López, Centro
Tel: 5518-3313
Metro: Salto de Agua and Bellas Artes
Open Monday-Saturday 7am-Midnight
Branches at Bolivar 58, Centro and Pennsylvania 73, Colonia Napoles
The original place, not far from the Mercado San Juan has been here since 1959, and was probably one of the first places in the city to serve *tacos arabe* or *al pastor*. Not your usual tacos, these

are rolled up and liberally bathed in a quite picante salsa. The newer branches are more spacious.

Taquería Arandas
República de Cuba 68, Centro
Open Monday – Saturday 9-9pm

A funky, old fashioned hole-in-the-wall, sporting aqua walls and a few folding tables, Arandas makes the best "tacos dorados" (a variation on flautas) that we have ever tasted. At 3.50 pesos per taco, a very cheap meal can be had here. Also available are carnitas, tortas and tepache from the barrel.

Taquería Tlaquepaque
Independencia 4, Centro
Metro: Bellas Artes
Open daily until 9pm

Although every kind of grilled meat taco is offered here, this large taqueria specializes in birria (lamb or goat cooked in broth with chili, see p.32): an order consists of 3 juicy tacos and a bowl of broth, served with good red or green salsa. *Aguas frescas* are flavorful. This is not a place for vegetarians.

La Texcocana (1936)
Independencia 8-A, near Balderas and the Museo de Arte Popular, Centro
Metro: Balderas, Juárez
Branch: Hamburgo 281, between Toledo and Sevilla, Zona Rosa
Metro: Sevilla

These are small bars with stools only that serve tortas. They offer a very unusual sardine torta, *queso fresco* with avocado (a good vegetarian option), and tortas of bacalao and carnitas.

Tortas El Cuadrilátero
Luis Moya 73, near Ayuntamiento, Centro
Metro: Juarez and Salto de Agua
Tel: 5521-3060
Open daily 10am-7pm

Owned by a retired wrestler named El Super Astro, this fonda specializing in tortas is decorated with lucha libre paraphernalia such as masks, photos and prizes. The torta "Gladiador" weighs 2 pounds; order it at your own risk. Other options are more reasonably sized, but are also large enough to share. *Antojitos* such as enchiladas and sopes are also available.

CONDESA / ROMA:

El "96"
Valladolid 96, Colonia Roma Norte
Metro: Insurgentes
Open Monday-Saturday Noon-6pm

Located between the Zona Rosa and Condesa, this
old-time fonda, decorated in retro white bathroom tile, is
a favorite of our friend Tomás and his hard-to-please mom.
The daily menu offers traditional dishes such as *puerco en
pipián, pechuga de pollo en mole verde, mole de olla* and *tortas de
camarón con romeritos*. It is reasonably priced, the portions are
generous, and the flavors authentic.

La Veracruzana - Fonda de Mariscos
Medellín 198B, corner of Chiapas, Colonia Roma
Tel: 5574 0474
open daily until 7
$

Located behind the Centro Comercial Plaza Insurgentes,
this charming little spot with an outdoor patio offers the
usual seafood options, i.e. ceviches, tostadas, filetes etc., but
does everything especially well and the prices are more tham
reasonable.

Taquería "El Greco"
Calle Michoacán 54 , 2 blocks from Parque México,
Condesa
Metro: Chilpancingo
Open Monday - Saturday 2pm-10pm

One of the owners is Polish, the others are Mexican and the
sign says *"tacos orientales."* Whatever the nationality, this
variation on *tacos al pastor* serves the spit-roasted and then

chopped meat (similar to shawarma or doneraki) both as tacos and in *pan arabe* (pita bread). The roasting aromas are sublime, as are the salsas. While there is often a wait for one of the few tables, you can eat standing up so you won't "*morirse de hambre*." The flan is also good. There is a branch called **Taqueraki** at Hamburgo 141 in the Zona Rosa.

El Jarocho (1948)
Manzanillo 49 corner of Tapachula, (behind the Sears, 1 block from Insurgentes), Roma
Tel: 5574-7148
Open Monday-Saturday 8am-10pm
Sunday 8am-7pm

Open since 1948, this restaurant offers a large range of classic tacos de guisado such as *carne de cerdo en salsa verde con verdolagas, pollo pibil,* and moles *verde* and *rojo.* While seemingly expensive at 18-24 pesos each, the tacos are large and come with two tortillas so it's really a 2-for-1 deal.

Taquería "El Guero" (Hola)
Avenida Amsterdam 135, near Michoacán, (across from the Superama), Condesa
Open Monday-Saturday 11am-6pm

This small taqueria, identified by its awning which states simply "HOLA", is renowned locally and has appeared in Saveur magazine. It serves our favorite *tacos de guisados,* with several vegetarian choices: try the cooked leafy greens *quelites* or *acelgas* (swiss chard) or *coliflór* (fried cauliflower.) The protocol is to order one at a time, and save your plate for more. Their *aguas frescas* are good too.

ZONA ROSA

Beatricita
Londres 190, between Florencia and Varsovia, Zona Rosa
Metro Sevilla
Tel. 5511-4213
Open Monday-Saturday for comida only

The legendary Taquería Beatriz on calle Rep. de Uruguay in the centro, founded by one Beatríz Muciño Reyes, was the oldest taquería in the country, celebrating its 100th anniversary in 2007; then promptly closing its doors. We still have Beatricita, albeit with a little less atmosphere, run by the same family, where the luscious moles poblano and verde are served in large yellow tortillas redolent of roasted corn that aficionados of the original will remember. There are lines at comida-time for the $56 peso menu.

COYOACAN:

La Barraca Valenciana
Centenario 91, Coyoacán
Tel. 5658-1880

This modest tortería, with a Spanish/Argentine influence, serves some unusual vegetarian choices of mushroom or eggplant tortas, as well as the house special, a torta of chopped calamar, dressed with chimchurri, the typical Argentine parsley garlic and olive oil sauce.

Other areas:

El Huarache Azteca (1940)
Torno 166, Colonia Artes Gráficas (not on map)
Metro: Jamaica
Tel:5768-4724, 5768-0320
Open Tuesday-Friday 7am-5pm , Saturday and Sunday 7am-2:30pm
Closed Mondays

The mercado Jamaica (see p.121) is famous for flowers and huaraches, not the ones you wear but the kind you eat. Huge, foot-shaped sopes piled with meat and/or cheese can be found at this popular place across the street from the market proper. Try the *pollo*, the *costilla* or the mole. Not for the grease-a-phobic, but worth the splurge in calories; a truly "authentic" experience. There can be lines to get in on weekends.

Los Sopes del 9
Luis Spota 85, 4 blocks from the metro stop,
Colonia Independencia (not on map)
Metro: Nativitas
Open until 8pm daily

In every neighborhood in the city are found mini-institutions, the "greats" that only the locals know about, until word gets out. This large, bustling purveyor of *sopes* is located south of the centro, a few blocks below the Nativitas metro stop on line 2. Their version of sopes is arranged from an ample assortment of ingredients, including, unusually, seafood. *Sopes de nopales* use a nopal cactus paddle as the bed for meat or cheese. There is a particularly large variety of *aguas frescas* available and the kitchen is open so you can see how they do it.

Tio Pedro
Antonio Caso 42 (between Insurgentes Nte. and Madrid
Colonia Tabacalera (not on map)
Open daily 24 hours

This ancient place, a few blocks north of Reforma, has blue
and white tile walls and groovy old signs. It is known for
its excellent *caldo de gallina* (chicken soup), accompanied by
hand-made tortillas and sopes, available round-the-clock.

El Borrego Viudo (1968)
Av. Revolución 241, corner of Viaducto, Colonia Tacubaya
(not on map)
Open daily 24 hours

This legendary taquería specializes in *tacos al pastor, de cabeza,
suadero,* and *tepache,* and if you are driving, has an enormous
garage where you can park and eat – good for a late-night/
early morning snack.

shucking oysters

RESTAURANTS: MEXICAN FOOD

RESTAURANTS: MEXICAN FOOD

In this chapter we list more formal restaurants that serve Mexican cuisine. A "restaurant" implies more service than a "fonda" but the range is wide. In this section are found restaurants specializing in regional cuisine as well. Most establishments in this category take credit cards.

CENTRO:

Cafe Tacuba (1912)
Tacuba 28
Metro: Allende and Bellas Artes
Tel. 5518 4950
Open daily 10am-10pm
$$

This traditional breakfast or after-theatre spot is a must-see; you don't know Mexico City if you haven't been to Cafe Tacuba. In business since 1912, the beautiful space is decorated in Talavera tiles and Colonial style furniture. The festive atmosphere includes strolling Estudiantina musicians who serenade families and tourists alike. The food, with many choices of Mexican classics, is more than satisfying and the Veracruz-style coffee is particularly good.

Chamula's Bar
Bolivar 438, corner of Torquemada, Colonia Obrera
(not on map)
Metro: José Peón Contreras
Tel: 5519-1336
www.chamulasbar.com.mx
Open daily 1pm-9pm
$$

Located a 15 minute taxi ride south of the Centro Histórico, this is one of the few places in the city specializing in the cuisine of Chiapas. Many unusual dishes are offered, such as *pozol,* a drink made with toasted corn and chili. Several moles and *pipianes, sopa de chipilín* (an unusual green herb) are other regional specialties. On weekends there is live music. It is worth a trip to this out-of-the-way neighborhood for those on the quest for authentic regional cooking.

Coox Hanal (1955)
Isabel la Católica 83, near Mesones, upstairs, Centro
Open daily 10:30am-6pm
$-$$

This is the best place for traditional Yucatecan cuisine; several of my friends have had their favorite meal in Mexico City here. Stick to the classics: *panuchos* (tortillas with black beans and cochinita pibil, a spicy shredded pork), *papadzules* (tortillas rolled up with chopped eggs and a green pumpkin seed sauce—a good choice for vegetarians), *pan de cazón* (tortillas layered with black beans, fish and tomato sauce), *sopa de lima* (chicken soup perfumed with special limes and fried tortilla strips), and horchata or a León or Montejo beer, direct from the Yucatán, to wash it all down. Be careful with the salsa of *chile habanero*: it is the world's hottest!

El Correo Español (1960)
Peralvillo 30, Centro (not on map)
Tel. 5529 0087 / 0397
Open daily, 12-9pm
$$-$$$

Located in the dicey Tepito neighborhood not far from La Lagunilla market, (i.e. be careful if you are walking there), this restaurant was founded by a Spanish immigrant as a cantina in the 1940's. Although there is an extensive menu of Mexican and Spanish favorites, it is a traditional place to eat *cabrito al horno*, (or roast baby goat) and is frequented by large families. A campy one-man orchestra provides background music to your meal.

Restaurante Lincoln (1935)
Revillagigedo No. 24, near Juárez, just south of the
Alameda, Centro
Metro: Bellas Artes, Juárez, Hidalgo
Tel: 5510-1468
Open Monday-Saturday 8am-8pm
Sunday 8am-6pm
$$

Conveniently located a few blocks from the Palacio de Bellas
Artes, this is an old-style Mexico City restaurant, where waiters
are older gentlemen wearing bow ties, and you are welcomed
with a dish of radishes and jícama when you sit down. Clubby
and slightly frayed at the edges, Lincoln was once a favorite
with politicians and artistes, and still offers courtly service and
delicious meals. The kitchen produces perfect renditions of
traditional dishes (*pipián verde, camarones con callo de hacha a
la marinera, chilpachole de jaiba*). For me, it's a quintessential
Mexico City experience.

Sanborn's (La Casa de Los Azulejos) (1917)
Calle Madero 4 corner of Eje Central, Centro
Metro: Bellas Artes
Tel: 5512-1331
www.sanborns.com.mx
Open daily 7am–1am
$-$$

Housed in an 18th-century mansion, this landmark is the
original of what is now a chain. A meal on the patio, with its
Art Nouveau murals, has been a beloved tradition since the
Sanborn brothers, American impresarios, opened their doors
in 1917. The food, best described as "Mexican institutional,"
is better than that at American chains and breakfast is quite
good. Be sure to make a trip to the bathroom to see the Orozco

mural painted in 1925. Branches all over the city have both stores and late night restaurants, but less charm.

Salón Victoria
López 43, corner of Victoria, Centro
Tel. 5512-9305 / 4340
Open Monday-Saturday 8am-8pm
$$

This cantina/restaurant, with old-fashioned décor, booths and service, is in the middle of the lighting district, a few blocks below the Alameda. It is a good place for *cabrito*, the house specialty. The large menu also includes unusually rich *sopa de ajo*, many typical Mexican dishes such as enchiladas, tortas and tacos and various daily specials.

Restaurante San Francisco
San Ildefonso 40, Centro
5702-9590 / 9110
Open Monday-Friday 9am-6pm
$$

This pretty restaurant in a colonial patio is probably the only one in the city that specializes in the cuisine of Tlaxcala. Located behind the Zócalo and very near the Museo de San Ildefonso, it is a peaceful respite from the hustle and bustle of the centro. Some unusual variations on pipian, mixiotes and cecina are on the menu as well as seasonal specialties.

Restaurante Bar Chon
Regina 160, several blockes east of the Zócalo, Centro, (not on map)
Tel. 5542-0873
Metro Pino Suarez
Open Monday – Saturday 1-6:30
$$-$$$

Although the publicity hypes the "prehispanic cuisine" at this famous institution, located near the Mercado Merced, the exotic dishes of ant eggs, grasshoppers, ahuautle (fresh water shrimp), armadillo, crocodile and wild boar are really modern concoctions utilizing ingredients once more commonly eaten, and often are more interesting for their shock value than their taste. That said, Chon prepares typical dishes not found on many menus and provides an opportunity for those who are less intrepid about eating in the market to try such things as pulque, *huazontles* or *cecina. Curados* (pulque sweetened with fruit) are offered as an aperitif, for example, and make a good accompaniment to the *panucho de salpicón de venado,* an open tostada topped with shredded and vinegared venison. The *sopa de migas,* really a garlic soup with bread, is light and satisfyingly garlicky. Fragrant and subtly flavored are the moles, green or red, served over duck, boar or plain old chicken. Traditional desserts such as the mysteriously named *flan imposible* or the *capoiritada* top off the meal. Service is friendly and helpful.

COLONIA CONDESA /ROMA:

La Bodega
Popocatépetl 25, corner of Av. Amsterdam, Condesa
Tel: 5525-2473, 5511-7390
www.labodega.com.mx
Open Monday-Saturday 1pm-1am
$-$$

This lively bar/restaurant/cabaret occupies a funky old Condesa mansion. Downstairs live music is featured (usually Cuban or jazz), and upstairs there is a small theatre where well-known cabaret performers entertain. This is the home base for Astrid Hadad, the "Mexican Bette Midler" – she has to be seen to be believed (www.astridhadad.com.) The food is good. We like to share the *plato de entremeses,* a plethora of Mexican *antojitos*, or the fish tacos. This is a great "anti-hip" place that will take you straight back to the Latin Quarter, Greenwich Village, or Berkeley in the early '60's even if you weren't born then. If you take your mother she'll want to get up and dance; and so will you.

Contramar
Calle Durango 200, near Plaza Cibeles, Roma
Metro: Insurgentes
Tel: 5514-3169
Open Monday-Saturday 1pm-6:30pm, Sunday 1:30pm-6:30pm
$$
Branch: Entremar
Hegel 307. Polanco
Tels: 5531-2031. 5531-7100

This fashionable spot (reservations are a must) is one of the best seafood restaurants in town. The large open room, simply but creatively decorated, has a bright, Pacific-coast beach atmosphere. The menu, designed by vivacious owner Gabriela Cámara, an advocate of the Slow Food movement (the tortillas are made from heirloom organic corn), is based on simple, fresh ingredients and is pure Baja: tuna sashimi and *pescado a la talla*, (a whole open fish grilled with two salsas–half red, half green) are outstanding. It is open for lunch only.

El Tizoncito (1966)
Tamaulipas 122 near Nuevo León, Condesa
Metro: Chilpancingo (several branches)
Tel: 5286-7321
www.eltizoncito.com.mx
Open Sunday-Thursday Noon-3am,
Friday, Saturday Noon-4am
$

This restaurant claims to have originated *tacos al pastor – quién sabe*? They were probably the first establishment to serve them in a restaurant setting. Whatever the case, this neighborhood institution does them very well; the *alambres* and side dishes such as salsas, *cebollitas* (small onions) and nopales are fine, as are the *aguas frescas*. This is a good first stop on arrival in Mexico or last stop after a late night out.

Flor de Lis (1918)
Huichapan 17, between Av. Amsterdam and Plaza Popocateptl, Condesa
Tel: 5286-0811
Open daily 9am-10pm
$

Well-known and beloved in the neighborhood, this place specializes in tamales. It is the only traditional Mexican restaurant in the Condesa. Breakfasts are especially good, the decor is drab but not unpleasant, and the prices are reasonable. It is located on a lovely, quiet street lined with Art Deco apartment buildings.

La Ostra
Nuevo León 109, Condesa
Tel. 5286-3319
Open Monday-Thursday Noon-8:30pm
Friday and Saturday Noon-10:30pm
$

The Condesa is full of pretentious and mediocre restaurants aimed at a young crowd but this is a great exception, not far from "restaurant row." A Pacific Coast style *marisquería*, this simple place has become something of a hangout for the "cool condechi" set. The blackboard menu includes *marisco* standards such as ceviche, and more unusual dishes like *aguachile de callo de hacha*, (scallops marinated in a lemony chili "water"), and tostadas of marlin, fresh and refreshing. There is a good tequila, mezcal and vodka selection. Highly recommended.

Pozolería Tizka
Calle Zacatecas 59, between Córdoba and Mérida, Roma
Metro: Hospital General
Open daily Noon-10pm
$

I used to live upstairs from this place, so I ate here a lot, always happily. They specialize in hearty and delicious *pozole verde*, a thick green soup from the state of Guerrero. It is similar to the red kind, but instead of tomatoes, ground pumpkin seeds thicken the soup base. Their tostadas are especially crisp, thick and redolent of corn. There is often live guitar music.

Tío Luís (1939)
Cuautla, at Montes de Oca 43, Condesa
Tel: 5553-2923
www.tioluis.com.mx
Open Monday-Saturday 1pm-11pm, Sunday Noon-7pm
$

This homey spot, which might remind you of an old neighborhood Italian trattoria, specializes in roast chicken, which is very good indeed, but also try the *milanesa* (veal cutlet) or the meatballs in chipotle sauce.

La Toma de Tequila
Toluca 28-C at Baja California
Metro Centro Médico (at the "Toluca" exit) (not on map)
Tel. 5584 5250
Open 1PM – 8PM Daily
$-$$

This freindly place specializes in the cuisine of Chihuahua, the northern state from which owner Raul Vargas hails – his wife is from Jalisco, which explains the incongruous use of "Tequila" in the name. Set in the second floor of an old house, the cheerful red and blue tablecloths, yellow walls, old wood floors and Northern-themed prints are warm and comforting. The menu features specialties of the region such as *asados*, meats prepared in a red "colorado" or green "pasado" sauce and served with large, fresh wheat tortillas. The *sopa de tortilla* is fragrant with cumin and served with *chicharrón*, avocado and roast chiles as a garnish, and the *frijoles norteñas* are garnished with queso Chihuahua, pungent fresh cheese and different chiles. The lemonade is rich and not too sweet, and deserts, such as Tequila flan are exceptional. Ask to sample their special house mezcal. No credit cards are accepted.

COYOACAN / SAN ANGEL:

El Morral (1967)
Allende 2, Coyoacán
Open daily 8:30am-8:30pm
$$

This large traditional Coyoacán restaurant, near the central plaza, is popular with families. It is good for breakfast and serves such classics as enchiladas *verdes, rojas* and mole. The decor is old fashioned and atmospheric, and the superior tortillas are made by hand within view of the diners.

See La Guadalupana (p. 113)

POLANCO / ANZURES

Los Panchos (1945)
Tolstoi 9, (not far from the Hotel Camino Real and the Parque Chapultepec museums), Colonia Anzures
Tel. 5254-5430
Open daily 9 AM - 10 PM
$$

This is a good choice for real traditional food and ambiance. Specializing in carnitas, which here are the best I have sampled in the city, everything else is also high up in its category: the hand-made tortillas, the salsas and the aguas preparadas.

SANTA MARIA LA RIBERA:

Pozolería La Casa de Toño
Sabino 144, two blocks from the Alameda of Santa María (not on map)
Colonia Santa Maria La Ribera
Metro: San Cosme
Tel: 2630-1084
Open Monday-Saturday 9am-11pm ,
Sunday until 10pm
$

Santa María La Ribera was the first colonia to be developed outside the centro in the mid-19th century. Now a working class area, much has been destroyed or left to deteriorate, but a few interesting monuments survive, such as the *museos* Chopo and Geología and the Kiosko Moro, a Moorish-style gazebo in the Alameda, or main plaza of the neighborhood. Two blocks from the plaza is the extraordinary Casa de Toño, a *pozolería* in a 19th-century mansion. Thick, red pozole with all the trimmings is the house specialty, although sopes, tostadas and other *antojitos* are also offered. At 34 pesos for a *grande,* this is a bargain meal. Lovely rooms decorated with murals and original mosaic floors come as part of the pleasant atmosphere.

La Oveja Negra
Sabino 215, Santa María la Ribera (not on map)
Teléfono: 5541 0405
Open Saturday and Sunday only
$$

This traditional neighborhood restaurant specializes in barbacoa, roasted in maguey leaves, which they only make on weekends and holidays. Everything here is of extra high quality, from tortillas to salsas - be sure to try the nopales aztecas as a side dish. Curados of pulque are on the menu as are several other antojitos for those who don't care for so much meat. Their sheep are raised organically on their own ranch, making this a true Slow Food gem.

ZONA ROSA / CUAUHTEMOC:

La Bella Lula
Río Lerma 86 (entre Río Rhin y Río Sena)
Colonia Cuauhtémoc
Tel: 5207-6356
Open daily 10am - 7pm
$$

Branches:
- Miguel Ángel de Quevedo 652, Coyoacán
- Corregidora no. 5, corner Av. Revolución,
  Colonia Tlacopac, (near San Angel)

Although Oaxacan cuisine is the most celebrated, talked and written about these days, it is hard to find the real thing in the capital. This popular restaurant around the corner from the Hotel María Cristina, has been serving authentic southern specialties since 1982 and does it very well. We sampled several of the moles: five of the famous seven Oaxacan moles are on the menu, and the almendrado stood out, sweet and tart yet complex and not overwhelming. A creative special was shrimp-filled nopales in black mole, and it worked. For a real taste of Oaxaca, don't miss the *tlayudas con asiento,* tender *tasajo* and *chapulines.* The tortillas and salsas are top notch; the ambience popular and festive.

Fonda El Refugio (1954)
Liverpool 166, near Insurgentes, Zona Rosa
Metro: Insurgentes
Tel: 5207-2732
Open Monday-Saturday 1pm-11pm
Sunday 1pm-10pm
$$

This classic restaurant serves Mexican standards in a lovely old house. Although it caters to tourists, you will find such authentic dishes as *manchamanteles* (pork with chili sauce and fruit) and various moles and pipians. The execution and presentation are exemplary and many Mexicans take their foreign visitors here. The menu is bi-lingual.

OTHER AREAS

Casa Merlos
Victoriano Zepeda 80, Colonia Observatorio (not on map)
Tel. 5277-4360
Open Thursday – Sunday 1-4pm
$$

Although located in a somewhat dreary neighborhood west of the centro, Casa Merlos is the best place to sample the regional cuisine of Puebla. The setting is rustic and homey - (stucco walls and red tile floors) in keeping with its traditional family-run history. Appetizers include chalupas, (or "little boats") a variation on the more common sopes. other worthwhile dishes are Manchamanteles (tablecloth stainers), a juicy stew of meat and dried and fresh fruit, pipian, and of course, the renowned mole poblano. Casa Merlos features several seasonal festivals; in October up to 10 different moles are offered.

Restaurante Arroyo
Insurgentes Sur 4003, Tlalpan (not on map)
Tel. 5573 4344
Open daily, 8am – 8pm
$$

Located in the southern end of the city, the largest restaurant in Mexico (if not the World!) with seating for more than 2000 people, is the ultimate Mexican experience. On weekends there are mariachis and it seems as if half the city is there. Although the menu is large and features just about every Mexican classic in the book, the specialty is country-style barbacoa.

Restaurant La Poblanita de Tacubaya (1947)
Luis G. Vieyra 12, Colonia San Miguel Chapultepec
metro Tacubaya (not on map)
Tel. 2614 4707
Open daily 9am-7pm
$

This lively and popular spot serves good Poblano specialties (from the state of Puebla). Sweet and chocolaty mole is, of course, featured, as are rich and nutty pipianes. Sopes or a caldo de gallina make good starters, and main course can be composed of tacos of the various guisados offered. A satisfying accompaniment is *arroz y plátanos*.

Don Polo (1958)
Felix Cuevas 86 (near Av. Coyoacán) Colonia Del Valle
Metrobus Felix Cuevas (not on map)
Tel. 5534 1805/5534-57
Open daily 7AM – 11:30PM
$

A beloved institution in Del Valle, this huge place serves great *tortas de pavo* (turkey) or *pierna* (roast pork) amongst others, accompanied by *licuados* made with your choice of fresh fruit. There is counter as well as take-out service.

El Gran Rábano (1957)
Victor Hugo 72, corner of Alhambra, Colonia Portales
(not on map)
Open daily from 7am
$

Originally a market stall, this large restaurant set in a garage-like space, specializes in pancita also called *menudo*, the rich broth of stewed tripe said to cure the worst hangover. Garnished with dried chilies, onion, lime and crumbled hierba santa (which supposedly helps with digestion), a bowl makes a hearty breakfast--if you can handle it. More antojitos are also on the menu.

La Polar (1934)
Guillermo Prieto 129, (between Velazquez De León & Melchor Ocampo, off of the Circuito Interior) Colonia San Rafael (not on map)
Metro Normal
Tel. 5546-2908 / 5546-5066
Open daily from 7am until midnight
$

"The best birria in Mexico" states the sign outside this large institution, located north of Colonia Cuauhtémoc, serving Doña Trini's original recipe of rich spicy birria from Jalisco. Two tacos, which are enormous, accompanied by a bowl of consomé, should do it for most people. There is live music on weekends.

Canto de Las Sirenas
Axayacatl 89 (off Circuito Interior, 3 blocks north of Av. Marina Nacional) Colonia Tlaxpana (not on map)
Metro Normal
Open daily 8am-9:30am
$

A well-known destination for *pescado y mariscos*, this enormous complex fills four large spaces. *Jaibas rellenas* (stuffed crabs), *mojarras*, and *sopa de mariscos* are the specialty; the *cocteles* are excellent and seafood is fresh. It is busiest on weekends.

NUEVA COCINA MEXICANA

LA NUEVA COCINA MEXICANA

Mexican cuisine has no high and low distinctions. In contrast to French, Chinese or Japanese cooking, the vast lexicon of Mexican recipes are culled from the humble traditions of everyday kitchens. The difference between "high" and "low" is a matter of the degree of luxury of the presentation rather than of the basic cooking concepts.

In recent years a culinary trend has emerged from the kitchens of a new generation of chefs and it is called *Nueva* or *Alta Cocina Mexicana*. Utilizing international culinary techniques, but working with traditional Mexican products and ingredients, these cooks have created a body of new recipes. For example, Patricia Quintana's salmon appetizer with vanilla-infused dressing uses traditional ingredients but all new cooking techniques.

And Mónica Patiño's *sopa de pollo perfumado con té de limón* includes lemongrass, sold in markets across the country, but not usually used in a dinner entree. Sometimes it is simply a matter of presentation and context: Martha Chapa's duck in black mole varies little from that eaten in an old Oaxacan home. But it is elegantly served on contemporary white china, in a streamlined Polanco venue, paired with less standard accompaniments, and chased with a nice Chardonnay. This cooking should not be compared to French Haute Cuisine; Mexican cooking crosses class lines—the idea of tortillas, or huauzontles or huitlacoche on a bourgeois table is what is new.

Azul y Oro
Centro Cultural Universitario, on the second floor above the bookstore (near Sala Nezahualcóyotl), Ciudad Universitaria (not on map)
Metrobus: Dr. Gálvez or Metro Universidad, then a short taxi ride
Metro: Universidad
Tel: 5622-7135
Open Sunday-Tuesday, 10am-6pm
Wednesday-Saturday 10am-8pm
(Hours vary from season to season, so check first)
$$

Chef and culinary investigator Ricardo Muñoz Zurita's restaurant, located on the UNAM (Autonomus University of Mexico) campus, is off the usual tourist path, but worth a detour. Featuring Oaxacan influences with a modern twist, the changing menu is varied and reasonably priced. Duck ravioli with mole and spaghetti with salsa de huitlacoche are two of his simple yet magnificent entrees. In addition to the regular menu there are seasonal and regional specialties. Desserts include a fabulous *tamal de chocolate con piña.* The hot chocolate from Oaxaca is the best we have ever tasted — a special mix of 70% chocolate and 30% almonds. Muñoz is the author of the *Diccionario Enciclopédico de Gastronomía Mexicana,* an indispensable work in Spanish covering every aspect of Mexican gastronomy.

El Bajío (1972)
Avenida Cuitláhuac 2709, Colonia Obrera Popular
Metro: Cuitláhuac (not on map)
Tel. 5234-3763.
Open Monday-Friday 10 am-6:30 pm,
Saturday, Sunday 9am-6:30pm
www.carnitaselbajio.com.mx
$$

Three Branches:
-Parque Delta Mall, Av. Cuauhtémoc 462,
Colonia Narvarte (not on map)
Tel. 5538-1188
Open Daily 8am-8pm

-Alejandro Dumas 7, Colonia Polanco
Tel. 5281-8245
Open Monday-Saturday 8am - 11pm, Sunday to 7pm

-Plaza Parque Reforma 222 (in a new high-rise at the
intersection of Reforma and Insurgentes)
Tel. 5511-9124, 5511-9117
Open Monday-Saturday 8am - 10pm, Sunday to 7pm

Chef Carmen Titita, author of several cookbooks, is
another big name in the Mexico City culinary scene. Her
original restaurant is popular with large families, especially
on weekends. The food is traditional and there are always
interesting choices:besides the popular carnitas, there is duck
in black mole and chongos (a weirdly wonderful curdled milk
dish) for dessert. Recently, three branches have opened: one at
Parque Delta, a sleek shopping center that is more accessible
to the Centro, but lacks the ambience of the original location.
Another branch in Polanco is more appealing and open at
night, the third, near Zona Rosa is also open late. The menu
in all three locations is the same.

El Cardenal (1969)
Three locations:
Palma 23, (between Cinco de Mayo and Madero), Centro
Metro: Zócalo
Tel: 5521-8815 / 8816 / 8817
$$-$$$

Juárez 70 (inside the Hotel Sheraton), Centro
Metro Juárez, Hidalgo
Tel: 5518-6632 , 6633

Palmas 215, Colonia Lomas de Chapaultepec
(not on map)
Tel: 2623-0401
www.elcardenal.com.mx
Open daily: 8am-7pm

The original restaurant, on Palma only a block from the
Zócalo, was for many years a rather stuffy, forgotten place.
Recently they have revamped the menu and become a good
venue for *nueva cocina*. Two larger branches have opened, one
in the Hotel Sheraton on the Alameda (built on the site of
the Hotel del Prado, destroyed in the earthquake of 1985), the
other in Lomas, west of the center. All three locations serve the
same changing menu offering many interesting dishes such
as *tortas de huautzontles, tortilla de huevo con escamoles* (ant
eggs), *esquites* (fresh corn), and many seasonal ingredients such
as huitlacoche and bacalao. The original Palma restaurant is
more old-fashioned and homey, while the new branches offer
contemporary glamour: take your pick.

El Tajín

Miguel Angel de Quevedo 687, (inside the Centro Cultural Veracruzano), Coyoacán.
Tel: 5659-4447 or 5659-5759
Open daily 1pm-6pm
$$

Owner Alicia Gironella d'Angeli, one of Mexico's foremost chefs and authors (she wrote the new *Larousse de la Cocina Mexicana* among other books) is an original and tireless promoter of Mexican cuisine. Her husband Giorgio d'Angeli is founder and president of Slow Food Mexico, an organization that has been instrumental in getting the cuisine of Mexico made a UNESCO Patrimony of Humanity. The restaurant serves creative but traditional food, mostly based on the cuisine of the state of Veracruz. We sampled an outstanding *mole de xico,* a light, fruity sauce served with duck on fragrant hand-made tortillas. Another excellent dish is *milanesa de pollo*, chicken rolled with fragrant *hoja santa* leaves into green and white spirals, that are poached and served with mole. Open for lunch only.

Hip Kitchen

Av. México 188, (near Av. Sonora) in the Hotel
Hippodrome, Condesa
Tel: 5212-2110
Open Monday-Saturday, 1pm-Midnight
$$$

The dining room of the boutique Hotel Hippodrome, located in a meticulously restored 1931 Art Deco building near Parque México, offers an interesting fusion menu designed by Mexican/American chef Richard Sandoval. The food is both delicate and hardy. Start with an order of *edamame* (fresh soy beans in their pod) sautéed with j*amón serrano*, and crunchy, lightly dressed *ensalada de calamar*. Next try the firm red snapper filet floating on a light guajillo chili broth, accompanied by a *flan de huitlacoche*; the *risotto de huitlacoche* captures that odd ingredient's mushroomy essence. The place is frequented by an arty looking young crowd and *"gente 'nice'"* from fancier neighborhoods. The room is small so reservations are recommended.

Izote
573 Mazaryk, Polanco
Tel: 5280-1671
Open Monday-Saturday 1pm-1am, Sunday 1pm-6pm
$$$

Owner/chef/author Patricia Quintana has pioneered the idea of *Nueva Cocina Mexicana.* Her restaurant has become a pilgrimage site for international food lovers— it's been written up in many culinary publications. The décor is simple, the service discreet. Quality can vary, but it always seems better when the owner is there, making the rounds and keeping an eye on her kitchen. Intriguing dishes include *lasagne de huitlacoche* and smoked salmon with avocado and vanilla. This is a good place to try such standards as *ensalada de nopales* or pozole. Desserts, especially the *pastel de mazapán* with almonds and white chocolate, are divine.

Pujol
Francisco Petrarca 254, Polanco
Tel: 5545-4111
www.pujol.com.mx
Open Monday-Saturday 1pm -11pm
$$$

Pujol is another of Mexico City's most talked about restaurants. Young chef and owner Enrique Olvera, recipient of Mexico's Chef of the Year Award, Wine Spectator's Award of Excellence, and the AAA Four Diamond Award, offers a unique and insightful approach to a fusion of European and Mexican cuisine. There is an a la carte menu, as well as a 5-course tasting menu and a 9-course chef's menu. The simple but elegant 55-seat room is comfortable, and the service is professional—everything you would expect at this level. The *cappuccino de flor de calabaza*, Olvera's contribution to the ever-growing "foam" lexicon, is very well done, a truly intelligent way to bring out the subtly elusive flavor of squash blossoms, the princess of Mexican ingredients. Also notable is the cacao encrusted venison. While certain dishes are truly unusual and surprising, others, interesting combinations of exotic ingredients in which no particular one stands out, are more elusive. Take the hyperbole with a grain of *fleur de sel* and go—you will not get as interesting a meal back home.

Solea
Campos Elíseos 252 (inside the W Hotel), Polanco
Tel. 9138-1818
Monday-Thursday 6:30am-12am, Friday, Saturday 6:30am-1am, Sunday 2-6pm
www.soleamexico.com
$$$

Executive Chef Eduardo Osuna creates interesting combinations, playing with classic Mexican ingredients and dishes. The dining room is as sleek and smartly lit, as one would expect it to be in the W Hotel.

Taberna del León

Altamirano 46, Plaza Loreto, Colonia Tizapan de San Ángel
Tel: 5616-3951
Open Monday-Saturday 2pm-10pm,
Sunday 2pm-6pm
$$$

Chef Mónica Patiño uses classic Mexican ingredients, sometimes in new ways, sometimes traditionally, ocasionally with an Asian touch. This comfortably elegant restaurant is located in an old mansion in Plaza Loreto, a former paper factory turned shopping center. The glassed-in patio is a romantic spot for an afternoon comida. Outstanding main dishes include *atún sellado con caponata y fettuccini* (tuna in an eggplant caponata) and *pato asado con vinagre balsámico, miel, ajonjolí y especias* (duck in a balsamic, honey, sesame and spice sauce). The salads are remarkable for their flavorful organic greens. This is a great choice in the south of the city.

Patiño is owner of two other popular and elegant restaurants that both feature Asian-fusion menus.

Naos, Palmas 425, Colonia Lomas de Chapultepec,
Tel: 5520-5702, and

MP Cafe Bistro, Andres Bello 10, Polanco,
Tel: 5281-0592

There is good live jazz at the bar here on Wednesdays

Paxia
Avenida de la Paz 47, San Angel
Tel. 5550-8355
Open Monday-Thursday 1pm-12am, Friday, Saturday 1-1am
Sunday 1-6pm
www.paxia.com.mx
$$$

Branches:
Juan Salvador Agraz, Santa Fe
Tel. 2591-0429

Paxia serves updated Mexican classics from various regions of
Mexico. The *pozole de mariscos* is a winner as are the *tacos de
pescado al pastor*. Flavored margaritas are also featured.

INTERNATIONAL CUISINE

INTERNATIONAL CUISINE

In this chapter we present a selection of restaurants of cuisines other than Mexican. As you would expect in a city of 25 million, there is a good range of foreign restaurants - the best food tends to be Spanish, while good Asian food is hard to find.

CENTRO:

Casino Español
Isabel La Católica 31, Centro
Metro: Isabel La Católica and Bellas Artes
Tel: 5512-9090
Open daily 1pm-6pm
$$

Housed in an ornate 19th-century edifice, this dining room is where the Spanish exile community recreates the old-world elegance of Madrid; it has the grandiosity of Paris without the pretension. Iberian standards such as *pimientos piquillos relleno de bacalao* (small sweet peppers filled with salt cod), *zarzuela de mariscos* (a seafood sauté) and, of course, paella (which in Mexico is rarely up to Valencian standards) are all superior. This is one of my favorite places to go in the city when I get nostalgic for the "old country." Weekend *comida* is popular with multi-generational families, and the daily *comida corrida*, at $10 US is a bargain.

Restaurante El Mesón Andaluz
Marconi . 3, corner of Donceles,
(next to the Museo Nacional)
Metro: Bellas Artes and Allende
Tel: 5510- 0787
Open daily 9am-6 pm
$$

This Spanish restaurant concentrates on the cuisine of Andalucia: classic dishes from southern Spain with a North African touch. *Salmorejo*, a dip of olive oil, tomato, garlic and bread, is just right—garlicky and fragrant with good olive oil. *Croquetas de bacalao* (cod cakes) are another Spanish classic well done. An *arroz negro* (rice cooked in squid ink) contains shrimps and other seafood, and is the best we have sampled outside of Spain. *Extraviado* (a white fish) *en salsa verde*, is prepared Basque-style, in a parsley-garlic olive oil sauce. There are many tempting tapas, several rice dishes, an abundance of seafood, and an intriguing *pollo Mosárabe relleno con frutos secos* (Mosarabic chicken stuffed with dried fruits.) The portions are enormous so most dishes can easily be shared. The space is comfortable, airy and light, although a bit generic in its bland decor, and unfortunately, marred by the addition of several glaring television sets.

CONDESA / ROMA:

Agapi Mu
Alfonso Reyes 96, Condesa,
Tel. 5286-1384
Open Tuesday-Saturday 1:30-11pm, Sunday, Monday 1:30-6pm
Metro Chapultepec
$$

Good Greek specialties such as paputsáka (stuffed eggplant), kalamárea (fried Greek-style squid), and dolmádes (stuffed grape leaves) are served in a pleasantly converted Condesa house with Mediterranean-style décor. There is live music weekends.

Bistro Mosaico
Michoacán 10, Condesa
Tel: 5584-2932
Metrobus: Campeche
Open Monday-Saturday 8:30am-11pm
Sunday Noon-5:30pm

Branches:

Av. de la Paz 14, San Angel
Tel: 5550-9778

Guillermo González Camarena 800,
Colonia Santa Fe, (not on map)
Tel: 5292-5326, 5166

Reforma 316, Zona Rosa, Colonia Juárez

This French-style bistro with a Spanish touch is one of the most fashionable spots in the Condesa. The chalkboard menu changes daily and offers eclectic choices such as lamb tajine, quiche aux morrilles, and celerie remoullade. The regular menu features such classics as onion soup and steak au poivre, but the Spanish influence is evident in dishes like arroz negro and various tortillas españolas. The atmosphere is jolly and there are tables outside if you don't mind the traffic. Also notable is the charcuterie takeout counter, the only one of its kind in the area, offering herring in curry cream, white bean salad, confit of tomatoes, terrines, quiches, and good French breads, all very reasonably priced. The breakfast is good as well.

Of dependably high quality, Mosaico is our favorite place in this neighborhood.

Bistro Rojo
Av. Amsterdam 71, Condesa
Tel: 5211-3705
Metrobus: Sonora
Open Monday-Thursday 2pm-11pm
Friday, Saturday 2pm-midnight, Sunday 2pm-6pm
$$

This bustling spot, with indoor and covered sidewalk seating, is one of a trio of bistros in the Condesa (see also Photo Bistro and Mosaico). The blackboard menu changes daily; good French standards such as leg of lamb, *magret de canard,* creative pastas, and large salads are offered. A changing house wine is available. The atmosphere and decor are Quartier Latin via New York's West Village. An unpretentious favorite of Condesa locals.

Casa D´Italia
Agustín Melgar 6, between Mazatlán and Pachuca, Condesa
Metro: Chapultepec
Tel: 5286-2021
Open Monday-Saturday Noon-11pm
$$

A small Italian place which is very popular with Condesa residents. The owner, Luigi, is from Naples —if you speak Italian, so much the better. The food is dependable and there are often specials not on the menu, but you need to ask. This is a good, intimate alternative to the larger *chi-chi* Condesa spaces.

Casita de Buenos Aires
Querétaro 188, two blocks from Av. Insurgentes, Roma
Metrobus: Sonora
Open daily 1:30pm-7pm
$$

Our Argentine neighbor Horacio recommends this authentic Argentine place as the best in the city. The walls are decorated with the jovial owner's Buenos Aires memorabilia, and especially good is the brochette of assorted meats, as well as the various lasagnas. The wine list includes an extensive Argentine selection.

El Jamil
Amsterdam 306, corner of Celaya, Condesa
Tel: 5564-9486
Metrobus: Sonora
Open Monday-Saturday 2pm-11pm,
Sunday 1pm-7pm
$$

This one of the best of several Lebanese places in the city. The decor is simple, the music authentic, and the sidewalk tables have views of tree-lined Avenida Amsterdam. The food is above average here, clean and fresh, and the bread is hot. A pleasant alternative in a quieter part of the Condesa.

Non Solo Pannino
Calle Orizaba, Plaza Luís Cabrera, between
Zacatecas and Guanajuato, Roma
Tel: 3096-5128
Open Monday-Saturday 1 pm-Midnight
Sunday 1pm-7pm
$

This simple, charming place has tables outside facing a leafy plaza with a fountain. The salads, made with quality ingredients, are filling. The *pannini* (pressed sandwiches) are excellent.

Photo Bistro
Plaza Citlatépetl 23 at Av. Amsterdam,
Condesa
Tel: 5286-5945
Metro: Chilpancingo
Open Monday-Saturday 2 pm-2am,
Sunday 2pm-7pm
$$

After 35 years, French photographer Christian Besson turned his studio into a restaurant, but kept the theme going with changing photography exhibitions. This hip but comfortable spot offers satisfying bistro classics—onion soup, good salads and my favorite, *bisque de mariscos*, a dense and satisfying soup.

Be sure to check daily specials on the blackboard. Well-chosen jazz is always in the background but not too loud, a real plus.

El Malayo
Plaza Rio de Janeiro 5, Colonia Roma
Tel. 5514 7686
$$-$$$

One of the best options in La Roma in a lovingly restored art-deco space. The meticulously prepared dishes reflect the multi-cultural cuisine of the chef who is from
Singapore, the original Asian-fusion country.

COYOACAN / SAN ANGEL:

Fiesole
Av. del Parque. 2   entrance on Av. Revolución, Colonia Tlacopac (across from the Centro Helénico, near San Angel)
Metro: Barranca del Muerto
Tel: 5663-1913
Open Monday-Thursday 2pm-11pm,
Friday-Saturday 2pm-Midnight, Sunday 2pm-7pm
$$$
Branch: Av. de las Palmas 555, Lomas de Chapultepec

This classy trattoria was recommended to me by my Italian teacher Elvis as the best Italian restaurant in the city. Set in a cozy grotto-like space, it features brick-oven pizzas, which I find to be dry and dull. Instead, I recommend their various creative pastas, such as *langosta al pesto*, (lobster with pesto) or *spaghetti al acciughe e sardine fresche,* (spaghetti with fresh anchovies and sardines). The *secondi* are interesting: we particularly liked the *venado en salsa de zarzamora,* (venison in blackberry sauce). Lamb is nicely prepared here. There is a good international wine list; reservations are recommended.

Trattoria della Casa Nuova
Avenida de la Paz 58-M, 2nd floor, San Angel
Metrobus: Altavista
Tel: 5616-2288
Open Tuesday to Friday 8 am-12 am, Saturday and Sunday,
9am-11pm, Monday for dinner only (bakery open all day)
$$-$$$

This trattoría is also a bakery, and both are of exceptional quality. The simple menu of pastas and pizzas offers classics, all very well done. The *spaghetti ai frutti di mare* is flavorful, the shrimps not overcooked and the pasta perfectly *al dente*; ditto the *spaghetti carbonara.* Salads are interesting, if not as generous as one would like: the gorgonzola is authentic, the greens a mixture of radicchio and leaf lettuce. Fresh, homemade breads are especially flavorful but the desserts are a little less exciting. The atmosphere is light and cheerful, service good, waiters cute. Ambient music on our last visit was provided by Rosemary Clooney and other beloved jazz divas, and at the right volume.

POLANCO / ANZURES:

Bellaria
Mazarik 514, Polanco
Tel: 5282-0413, 0414
www.bellaria.com.mx
Open Monday-Saturday 1:30 pm-Midnight
Sunday 1:30pm -5pm
$$$

Bellaria is a comfortable, dependable Italian restaurant complete with wood burning pizza oven. Recommended specials are *lasagnetta Bellaria* (filled with duck and artichoke), *salame di polpo Bellaria* ("salami" of octopus finely sliced and dressed with olive oil and lemon), and the *pizza a la leña.*

Benkay Restaurant

Hotel Nikko, Campos Elíseos 204,
Polanco
Tel: 5280-1111
Open Monday-Friday 7am-10:30am, 1pm-5pm, 7pm-11pm;
Satuday 1pm-11pm, Sunday buffet, 1pm-5pm
$$-$$$

This Japanese restaurant is noteworthy for its Sunday brunch buffet with its ample selection of seasonal dishes, all of high quality and authentic in flavor and preparation. I have sampled dishes such as oden (stewed winter vegetables) and seaweed salads, which I haven't seen outside Japan. The sushi selection is limited but good and tempura is brought out in small quantities so that it is always fresh. This place is frequented by Japanese families, a sure sign of authenticity. The atmosphere is typical of many Japanese dining spots, with separate booths and tatami rooms. At about $22 US, this is one of the great dining bargains in the city. Reservations are highly recommended. The regular menu is pricy but good.

Biko

Presidente Masaryk 407, Polanco
Tel. 5282-2064
Open Monday to Saturday 1:30-11pm
http://www.biko.com.mx
$$$

Young chefs Mikel Alonso and Bruno Oteiza, formerly of Tezka and trained in Arzak, the temple of Gastronomy in Northern Spain, have opened an elegant spot called Biko, which means "couple or "duo" in Euskara, the language of Basque Spain. It features two menus, one traditional and the other "evolutionary" i.e. more creative. All the dishes we have sampled are fresh and subtly flavored; recent standouts were: *alcachofas con almejas*, the Basque classic reinterpreted: a tender artichoke heart was wrapped in a lightly spiced batter and nestled and nestled in a fresh clam shell- the reduced broth made me want to lick the plate. Also good were the traditional *pimientos piquillos rellenos de bacalao*, whose balance of sweet and salty was nearly perfect, a creative *caldo de guisantes trufado y callo de hacha* a light pea soup perfumed with truffle oil and host to several succulent scallops swathed in cloaks of thinly cut mushroom, and the *escolar verde apio*, a grilled white fish in a simple sauce of reduced poultry stock with a hint of celery. Less successful was a lamb with a "toque Oriental" whose un-integrated shaving of cilantro seeds did not add the intended Asian touch to the rather bland piece of meat. The service is attentive and gracious, wine list extensive and reasonable, with many unusual (for Mexico) Spanish wines listed. The tasting menu, at around $60 US or $110 with "maridaje" of wines, is highly recommended. Biko is among the best restaurants in Mexico City.

Casa Portuguesa
Emilio Castelar 121, between Anatole France &
Oscar Wilde, Polanco
Open Monday- Wednesday 8am - 10:30pm, Thursday - Saturday 8am- 11:30pm, Sunday 9am - 6pm
Tel. 5281-0075
$$$

The only Portuguese restaurant in the city has tables overlooking the park and does several excellent bacalao dishes. There is live Fado music on weekends.

Le Cirque
Hotel Camino Real, Mariano Escobedo 700,
Tel: 5263-8888
Open Monday-Friday 1 pm-Midnight
Saturday 7pm-1am, Sunday Noon-5pm
$$$

Yes, this is the same Le Cirque as in New York with its classy look of international glamour and with the expected circus touches. The menu includes some dishes well known from the original Manhattan location, such as pasta primavera, and a few creations featuring Mexican ingredients. Prices are considerably less than in its U.S. counterparts. A warning: this is probably the only restaurant in this book with a dress code, jacket and tie for men.

D.O.

Hegel 406, Polanco
Tel. 5255 0612, 0912
Metro Polanco
Open Monday – Saturday 2PM-2AM, Sunday 1:30-5PM
www.denominaciondeorigendo.com
$$$

D.O. is short for *denominación de origen*, the Spanish designation for distinctive regional foods. The menu, designed by master Basque chefs Pablo San Román and Bruno Oteiza, formerly of Tezka, is based on Spanish classics, concentrating on the Pais Vasco or Basque country: starters, (which can also be ordered as tapas, include *rabo de toro*, (a stew of ox-tail), *croquetas*, piquillo peppers stuffed with bacalao, and a good selection of Spanish hams. Main courses include many dishes from regional Spanish menus: *Kokotxas con gulas* (cod cheeks with eels, a Basque classic), *chipirones en su tinta* (small squids in their own ink), *conejo confitado en cava* (from Catalonia) and *chuleton* (a big juicy steak popular in Castile), and an excellent *solomillo* (like filet mignon).

The front dining room is open and sunny, inside it is darker and intimate, more reminiscent of a typical Spanish venue.

Jaso

88 Newton, Polanco
Tel. 5545 7476
Open Monday-Saturday: 2pm-11:30pm
www.jaso.com.mx
$$

The self-proclaimed "Contemporary American" restaurant Jaso is really Mexico's answer to the Ferran Adrià / El Bullí mania that has turned the culinary world upside down in recent years. Chef Jared Reardon (formerly of New York's Bouley and Daniel) and his wife, master pastry chef Sonia Arias, have created a superb gastronomic temple, featuring local, seasonal and organic raw materials. Foams, vegetable and fruit reductions and other already well-worn standards of "molecular gastronomy" are used intelligently and discreetly here. Oriental influences are evident, but one does not get the impression of "Asian-fusion" for the sake of trendiness.

On a recent visit, an ameuse-bouche "cappuccino" of almond scented with mint, was served in a martini glass, with little cubes of beet jello waiting as a surprise at the bottom. The confit of baby octopus, served on a bed of piquant eggplant puree, was tender and flavorful. The succulent lechón (suckling pig) was beautifully complimented by a beet reduction sauce. A second appetizer of grilled skate was highlighted by tiny diced pineapple and the brown sauce traditionally served with Japanese eel--a simple and beautiful treat. Sea-bass with puree of wild mushrooms was an odd, but successful combination. Chocolate brioche topped with a crispy orange cookie lid was as rich as it sounded and looked. Piping hot madeleines added a Proustian reflection on all things good, present and past. Presentation is simple – no food architecture, thank goodness and service is expertly knowledgeable and discreet. The décor is modern and sleek without being cold.

Au courant, hip and smart, Jaso is one of the city's best restaurants.

O'Mei
Hotel Nikko, Campos Elíseos 204
near Andres Bello, Polanco
Tel: 5281-6828
Monday-Saturday 1:30pm-5 pm
Sunday and Holidays Noon-5pm
$$

The Pan-Asian buffet lunch here is extensive, and at about $22 US, quite a good deal. Among the *"más de 100 platos exóticos"* are, naturally, winners and losers (I skip the cold fried things), but any Asia-phile will be happy with the roast Peking duck, the steamed dim-sum, Japanese salads, Vietnamese summer rolls, and a few good stir fried dishes. For dessert, bananas in coconut milk looks unappetizing but tastes great. The atmosphere is airy and pleasant.

SANTA FE / LOMAS:

La Mar Cebichería
Salvador Agraz 37, Colonia Santa Fe (not on map)
Tel: 5292-9776,
Open Sunday-Wednesday 1pm-6pm
Thursday and Saturday 1pm-11pm
$$$

Branches:
Av. Palmas 215, Lomas de Chapultepec, Tel. 5202-7500
Plaza Loreto, Tizapan, San Angel Tel. 5616-5249

La Mar founder Gastón Acuria is a big name in Peru; his "Astrid y Gastón," Lima's temple of High Andean fusion cuisine has received international acclaim. His restaurant, on the western edge of the city, offers many Peruvian standards. In addition to various ceviches are tacu tacu, (a rice and bean mixture topped with seafood), *saltados*, (dishes cooked in a wok—there is much Chinese influence in Peruvian cooking), rice dishes and grilled fish. The menu is almost entirely seafood; there are, unfortunately, no vegetables or salads of any sort. Quality is very high, and recipes are authentically Limeño, as are the pisco sours, the national cocktail, which is similar to a margarita. Please note that portions are large, and many dishes can easily be shared. The room, upstairs in a new high-rise, looks out onto the skyscrapers of Santa Fe—you'd think you were in Tokyo.

See **Bistro Mosaico** p. 86

ZONA ROSA / CUAUHTÉMOC:

Bistrot Arlequin
Río Nilo 42, Colonia Cuauhtémoc
Tel: 5207-5616
Open Monday-Saturday 1:30pm - 2am
$$$

This charming corner restaurant is a true French bistro. The small kitchen is open to the dining room. The limited menu offers *grande-mere* classics; the *quenelles*, a house specialty, are as light and fragrant as they should be and a salad with magret is well dressed and a decent size. On the blackboard menu, recently, was a *tarta de calabaza* (a simple salmon filet) and *pollitos en salsa de ciruela pasa,* (small chickens in a plum sauce). Several standard preparations of beef filets (*au poivre, moutarde*) are available with their requisite *pomme frites*, and of course, there is the ubiquitous *crème brûlée* for dessert. There is an ample wine list. With only a dozen tables, the place fills up with local business people so reservations are a must.

El Dragón

Hamburgo 97, corner of Genova, Zona Rosa
Tel: 5525-2466
Open Monday-Saturday 1pm-11pm,
Sunday 2pm-10pm
$$

Given the scarcity of good Chinese restaurants in the city, this
spot is a find. Known for its roast duck, El Dragón also serves
good hot and sour soup, General Tso's chicken and other
Chinese standards.

Biwon Korean Restaurant

Florencia 20, upstairs, Zona Rosa
Metro: Sevilla
Tel: 5514-3994
Open daily 10:30 am -11pm
$$

There is a large community of Koreans in the city, congregated
around the western edge of the Zona Rosa. Several restaurants,
clubs, stores (my favorite is at Hamburgo 214-A; they make
fresh tofu daily), even an acupuncturist (Cda. de Varsovia
10) can be found here. This restaurant, light and airy, is one
of the best. The menu is authentically Korean - your best
bet is to point to what other people, invariably Koreans, are
eating, or try to explain what type of dish you want. The
banchan (appetizers) are varied and satisfying. There are the
usual barbequed meats, casserole dishes such as a kim chi with
seafood and tofu, and various stir fries.

Tezka

Amberes 78, Zona Rosa
Metro: Insurgentes
Tel: 5228-9918
Open Monday-Friday 1pm-5pm and 8pm-11pm, Saturday 1pm-5 pm, closed Saturday evenings and Sunday
$$$

Branch:
 - Periferico Sur 4363 (Hotel Royal Pedregal), Pedregal (not on map)
Tel: 5449-4000
Open Sunday-Tuesday 1:30pm-5pm, Wednesday-Friday 1:30pm-11pm

Tezka is arguably the best restaurant in Mexico City. The menu, originally designed by the celebrated Basque chef Juan Mari Arzak, offers food that is innovative and inspired, combining local seasonal ingredients in inventive, but unpretentious ways. A foamy infusion of chayote, *sopavieja de xtipirones* (tiny, marinated calamares in a rich, brown meat stock) or *cordero en salsa de café* (a lamb filet wrapped in coffee leaves and flavored with a light infusion of coffee) are among the noteworthy offerings on the constantly changing menu. Though low on atmosphere - the Zona Rosa location is a bland hotel dining room - the servers are attentive and knowledgeable, able to answer any questions about the dishes, and there is a good, reasonably priced selection of Spanish and Mexican wines. The tasting menu, at about US $60 is a deal. Highly recommended for a splurge that, by many standards, is really a bargain

OTHER AREAS:

Ka Won Seng Restaurante Chino
Albino Garcia 362, corner of Av. Santa Anita,
Colonia Viaducto Piedad (not on map)
Metro: Viaducto
Tel: 5538-2368
Open daily until 11pm
$$

A true ethnic restaurant that is both run by and frequented
by non-Mexicans is still an oddity in this city. "Discovered"
by a friend via a taxi driver whose sister-in-law is Chinese,
this place has an extensive menu that caters to the local Asian
population. Chow mein, sweet and sour dishes, and coffee
and sweet rolls are the order of the day at most *restaurantes
chinos* in Mexico City, but not here! In fact, a sign taped in
the window declares "*No hay comida Mexicana, café, ni pan
dulce*" ("We don't serve Mexican food, coffee or sweet rolls").
Many unusual Chinese dishes are offered such as sea bass with
ginger and scallions, tofu casserole with eggplant, cold beef
with star anise, and fresh sautéed mustard greens, and all are
excellent. The decor is true to the genre, that is, non-existent.
The location is a bit out of the way, but this restaurant is worth
the trip if you crave "real" Chinese food.

DESSERTS
AND
CAFÉS

DESSERTS AND CAFES

CHOCOLATE AND CHURROS

Churrería el Moro (1954)
Eje Central Lázaro Cárdenas 42, between Uruguay and
Venustiano Carranza, 4 blocks down from the Torre
Latinoamericana, Centro
Metro: San Juan de Letrán, Salto de Agua
Open daily 24 hours
$

This classic *chocolatería* was recommended to me years ago
by the late Josefina Howard of New York's Rosa Mexicano
restaurant as one of her favorite places; it quickly became
one of mine. The concept of *churros y chocolate* is based on
a Spanish tradition celebrated in the ancient Churrería San
Ginés in Madrid. Four types of chocolate are offered: Español,
thick and sweet, Francés, rich but less sweet, Especial, sweeter
and classic Mexicano, flavored with cinnamon. And of course,
there are the churros, which are extruded out of the amazing
machine in the window, then deep fried and sprinkled with
sugar. Go after a concert at Bellas Artes or a drag show at
Buttergold's.

Chocolatería Mamá Sarita
Juan de la Barrera 1-D, Condesa
Tel: 5553-1362
Metro: Chapultepec
Open daily 10 am-11pm
$

Located in the infamous Edificio Condesa (known to locals as
"Peyton Place" because of the scandals caused over the years by
its bohemian residents), is this small chocolatería. The cacao,
grown by the owner, *Tabasqueño* Evelio Arias, and ground

on the premises is prepared in the traditional way, with a wooden beater, and served in the classic ceramic mug from Jalisco. Many desserts, such as *pan de elote* (sweet cornbread), are made by old ladies from the neighborhood. The fact that Mamá Sarita is officially gay-friendly is another plus.

Also serving similar fare until late at night:

Churrería del Convento
Plaza del Carmen 4, a block north of the Museo del Carmen, San Angel
Tel: 5616- 0978
Metrobus: La Bombilla
Open Monday-Saturday 8 am-1am, Sunday 8am-Midnight
$

Chocolate y Churros La Parróquia
Corner of Centenario and Xicotencatl, 2 blocks form the main plaza of Coyoacán

GELATERIAS

Gelaterías and *heladerías* are ice cream parlors.

Alto Tango
Musset 3, corner of Masaryk, Polanco
Tel: 5282-2020
Open daily 8 am-11pm
$

An *heladería Argentina*, the Buenos Aires version of an Italian gelatería, Alto Tango has the best ice cream I've had in Mexico, hands down. The *dulce de leche*, dark and burnt-sugary tasting, is superb, as are the dark chocolates. An outdoor *terazza* makes this a pleasant stop while strolling in Polanco. It's almost always full, but worth the wait.

Neveria Roxy (1944)
There are two branches near each other in the Condesa:
Av. Mazatlán 80, corner Fernando Montes de Oca
Av. Tamaulipas 161 corner Alfonso Reyes
Open daily 11am-8pm
$

"Any place called 'Roxy' has to be good," said our friend Karen. This old soda fountain, the kind all but extinct in the United States except as a retro recreation, miraculously preserves the classic Formica bar and milkshake mixers. Known to several generations of *Condechis* (as Condesa residents are locally called), the ice cream, banana splits, and sodas are good, although the *malteadas* don't have malt in them any more.

La Bella Italia (1922)
Orizaba 110 at Alvaro Obregón, Roma
Metro: Insurgentes
Open daily 10am-9pm
$

If the Roxy might have been the haunt of Judy and Mickey, La Bella Italia, with its '50's jukebox, is pure James Dean. Despite the name, the ice cream is more American than Italian style, but the flavors are well defined.

Gelatería Neve & Gelato
Cuernavaca 124, near Michoacán, Condesa
Tel: 5255-3345
Open daily 8:30am-11pm
$

Branch: Parque Luís Cabrera, (Orizaba & Zacatecas), Roma
In the heart of the Condesa, this is a good people-watching place with sidewalk tables and familiar ice cream concoctions.

CAFES

La Balance Pâtisserie
Cozumel 94 A, at Sonora, facing Parque España,
Condesa
Open daily 9am-8pm
$

This small café has very good pastries and is frequented by knowledgeable Europeans. There are a few tables, or you can order *para llevar* and sit in nearby Parque España.

Maque
Ozulama 4 at Parque México, Condesa
Tel: 2454-4662
Open daily 8am-10pm
$-$$
Branch: Emilio Castelar 209, Polanco

Start a tour of Colonia Condesa with breakfast at this lovely Viennese-style indoor-outdoor café with a view of Parque Mexico. The menu is a glossary of Mexican breakfast dishes and the homemade pastries and coffee are good.

Café Jekemir (1945)
Isabel la Catolica 72, near Mesones, Centro
Metro: Isabel la Catolica
Tel: 5709-7038
$

Forget those ubiquitous Seattle-based chains. I make a trip to this place in the Centro to buy my Veracruzano coffee beans; they are the best as well as the cheapest. You can also sit here to have a cup of coffee and your choice of Middle Eastern pastries. Owned and run by several generations of a Lebanese family, it has become a hangout for classical musicians.

Café La Habana (1960)
Morelos #62 at Bucareli , Centro
Tel. 5534-2620 / 5546-0255
Open Monday-Saturday 7am-11pm, Sunday, 7-10pm
$

This huge cafe is located a few blocks south of the Alameda and is known as a hangout for journalists who work at the nearby offices of most of the large dailies. The food is nothing to write home about but the coffee is good.

Caravanserai Maison Francaise de Thé
Orizaba 101-A, near Casa Lamm, Roma
Open Monday-Friday 10am-9:30pm, Saturday Noon-9:30pm, Sunday 3pm-9:30pm
$

This cute tea salon has cozy seating areas each with an appealingly different and eclectic decor. They also sells loose teas and tea paraphernalia.

CANTINAS, BARS AND PULQUERIAS

CANTINAS, BARS AND PULQUERIAS

There is not much difference between a bar and a cantina, although the latter implies a simpler, humbler place, like a pub. There are lots of historic cantinas and bars with interesting atmosphere, especially in the Centro. Some of these serve food or even have free appetizers. We list these as well as contemporary alternatives.

CENTRO:

Bar La Opera (1870)
Cinco de Mayo 10, Centro
Tel: 5521-8375
Metro: Bellas Artes, Allende
Open Monday-Saturday 1pm-Midnight, Sunday 1pm-6pm
$

How can we not mention the famous Bar La Opera with its bullet hole from Pancho Villa's gun? Belle Epoch has never been more "belle" than here and this has been an obligatory stop for generations of visitors. Don't eat dinner here, just order an appetizer, as the food is standard.

Cantina La Montañosa (1948)
Calle Palma, corner of Cerrada de 5 de Mayo (between 5 de Mayo & Tacuba), Centro
$

This traditional cantina, dating from 1948, serves free botanas, or small dishes (often quite filling) to accompany the drinks, from 2-5. With one drink you are offered a mouthwatering range of seafood dishes such as ceviche, avocado stuffed with tuna or huachinango a la Veracruzana (there a two drink minimum for all-you-can-eat). Lunch can be had standing at the bar or seated in the dining room upstairs.

La Puerta del Sol
Cinco de Mayo, corner of Palma, Centro
Metro: Allende, Bellas Artes, Zócalo
$

The original Art Deco doors swing open to welcome you to this old fashioned cantina. It's a miracle that it has survived right in the center of the city! Botanas (hors d'oeuvres) are offered with drinks during the day.

El Tio Pepe (1870)
corner of Independencia and Dolores, Centro
Metro: Bellas Artes and Salto de Agua
Tel: 5512-7844
$

In Mexico City many old places have been preserved simply because nobody ever thought to change them; they are authentically old and do not have a "Disney-fied" restored look. This old cantina, with its original Art Nouveau bar has been the scene of many political discussions over the years. It is a good alternative to the more touristy and expensive Bar Opera. During the day free botanas are served. If you're lucky you'll get a booth.

Salón Corona (1928)
Bólivar 24, Centro
Metro: Bellas Artes, Allende
Tel: 5512-5725
Open daily 8 am-1am
$

This unpretentious place has been feeding taco eaters since 1928. There are two bars: one for *tacos de guisados,* offering a nice variety of seafood options such as bacalao and *pulpo* as well as mole verde and *picadillo*; the other bar is for *cocteles de mariscos*. Beer is cold and on tap, unusual in Mexico, order it "*de barríl*". Corona provides a good quick refueling station during your sojourn through the Centro Historico. There is also a large dining room with waiter service, and a very mixed crowd (in class and age) has re-discovered this, one of the few surviving *cervecerias* in the Centro.

Zinco Jazz Club
Motolinia 20 (basement), Centro
Metro Bellas Artes, Allende
Tel: 5512-3369
Open Wednesday-Sunday, from 9pm
www.zincojazz.com.
$$

The best jazz club in the city is in the basement of an Aztec-Deco office building and will remind jazz lovers of the Village Vanguard in New York. Good local groups headline; check their webpage for schedule.

Papa Beto Jazz Bistro
Manuel Villalongín 196-H near Rio Tiber
Colonia Cuauhtémoc (not on map)
Tel: 5592-1638
www.papabeto.com
$$

Another jazz venue that offers excellent local musicians in a fun, funky, acoustically superior space.

CONDESA / ROMA:

Bar Cibeles
Plaza Villa de Madrid 17, Roma
Tel: 5208-2029, 1456
Open Tuesday-Saturday 7pm- 2am
$$

Located near the fuente de Cibeles (which has been trying hard to gussy itself up with mixed success), this self-styled retro bar, which has the same owners as Contramar, around the corner, is a good place for a drink and a light snack such as pizza if you are in the mood for an L.A.-like experience and a little "ambiente cool." A large space with tables and a long bar, it gets quite busy on weekends.

Condesa DF
Veracruz 102 at Parque España, Condesa
Tel: 5241-2600
Open Sunday-Wednesday 7pm-Midnight
Thursday-Saturday 7pm-1:30am
$$$

The visiting artistes and frivolous (such as a certain silly hotel-chain heiress who needs no more ink spilled in her name) like to stay at the Condesa DF, and since such people don't sleep much, the noisy rooms must not bother them. For the rest of us, the rooftop terrace bar is a great spot for a drink and an hors d'oeuvre. If you can be there at sunset, so much the better. Call for reservations.

Covadonga
Puebla 121, Colonia
Tel: 5533-2701
Metro: Insurgentes
Open Monday-Saturday 1pm –2am
$

This traditional club for Spanish ex-patriots has, for some reason, become a hangout for artists, but the old-timers can still be found sitting around shmoozing in the vast, flourescent-lit room. There is a good wine list, but don't be tempted by the food, which is mediocre at best. Stick to basic tapas like *bocadillos*, *tortilla española*, or *calamares a la Romana*.

La Botica Mezcalería
Campeche 396, Condesa
Tel: 5521- 6045
Open daily 5pm-2am
$

Mezcal is a liquor similar to tequila, but with a bad reputation, because much of what was produced in the last 100 years was rotgut. It has recently made a comeback as a refined beverage through efforts to promote good, aged mescals. The bottle with the worm is getting to be a chic alternative to tequila. This small bar offers a large selection in a pleasant setting.

Tierra de Vinos
Durango 197, near Plaza Madrid, Roma
Metro: Insurgentes
Tel: 5208-4822
$$

Branch: Juan Salvador Agraz 60, Colonia Santa Fe

Tel: 5292-2984
Open Sunday-Tuesday 1pm-5pm, Wednesday-Saturday 1pm-Midnight

These elegant but pricey wine bars offer an impressive selection of wines from around the world. Spanish style tapas are offered.

Also see **La Bodega**, (p. 59)

COYOACAN / SAN ANGEL

La Guadalupana   (1932)
Higuera 14, near the central plaza, Coyoacán
Tel: 5554-6542
Open Monday-Saturday 1pm-11:30pm
$

Everyone knows that Frida, Diego and Trotsky partied here. But unlike the equivalent Hemingway hangouts in Paris, La Guadalupana has not become an overpriced tourist trap; it retains its old-fashioned working class charm, bullfighting décor and experienced service. Botanas are offered with drinks and there is a serviceable menu of Mexican standards.

San Angel Inn
Diego Rivera 50, San Angel
Tel: 5616-2222
Open Monday-Saturday 1pm-1am, Sunday 1pm-10pm
$$

There's not much to say about the food at this venerable institution set in an old hacienda, but the patio is lovely and, according to some, they make the best martinis in the city. It is well worth a look for the appealing colonial ambiance.

POLANCO / ANZURES:

Blue Lounge
Hotel Camino Real, Mariano Escobedo 700,
Colonia Anzures
Tel: 5263-8888
Open daily
$$

When you've had it with vintage, go to this bar that features a glass floor over a shallow pool; it is the place to wear your Prada shoes and Little Black Dress. Located in the lobby of the Legoretta-designed Camino Real Hotel, it is truly glamorous— and you could continue upstairs to Le Cirque (p.94.)

Terraza-bar Área Hotel Hábita
Calle Lamartine 347, Polanco
Tel: 5280-0231
Open Monday-Saturday from 7pm
$$

Atop the highly designed Hotel Hábita, this open-air terrace is peaceful, chic, and very popular, although it feels more like L.A. than Mexico. They feature drinks with funny names: order them at your own risk.

SANTA MARIA LA RIBERA:

Salón París (1950)
Torres Bodet 152, corner Salvador Díaz Mirón (not on map)
$

At the corner of the Alameda of Santa Maria la Ribera, this traditional cantina is supposedly the place where ranchera giant José Alfredo Jiménez got his start singing in public. It is a favorite with locals and still offers live traditional music. Free "*botanas*" come with the drinks, an old tradition which lives on here. I put "*botana*" in quotation marks because I was served a large plate of succulent *pulpo a la veracruzana*, with rice and bolillos, as well as cucumber and jicama, then offered a *queso fundido* which I had to refuse, all for the price of a beer.

PULQUERIAS

Pulque, made by fermenting the fresh sap of the maguey cactus, has a thick texture and a yeasty taste. *Curados* are sweetened pulques that have been flavored with fruits, vegetables, or nuts. Pulque was used in Aztec rituals and has long been considered a drink of the common man. It is usually served only in pulquerías, which had been slowly disappearing but seem to be making a comeback as fashionable places for young people to meet. Pulquerías have erratic hours but are generally open from about 9am to 8pm and are closed Sundays. Prices are low, usually 9 or 10 pesos for a *vaso*, 14 or 15 for a *tarro* or mug.

La Hortensía
Callejón de la Amargura # 4 Plaza Garibaldi, Centro
Metro: Garibaldi

A popular pulqueria on the Plaza Garibaldi about 5 blocks north of the Alameda on Eje Central, where you can sit at an outdoor table and listen to the cacaphony of dozens of strolling mariachi bands while sampling various *curados* and *botanas*. This is a dicey area so don't go alone and do watch your wallet. There is a *sitio* (taxi stand) in front for a safe ride home.

Other pulquerías are:

La Antigua Roma
Allende corner of Republica de Perú, Centro
This is a rather down and out place, not for the faint hearted.

La Xochitl
Ancona between Bodet and Naranjo, Santa Maria La Ribera

La Risa (1901)
Calle Mesones 71, a few blocks from the Zócalo, Centro
Metro: Zócalo, Pino Suarez

La Risa is probably the oldest operating pulqueria in the city. On our last visit we witnessed a house full of wholesome students having a good time while a bemused long-time waitress and a couple of old-timers looked on.
Enjoying pulque

Enjoying pulque

SHOPPING

SHOPPING

MARKETS

In Mexico City neighborhoods, the tall red and green *Mi Mercado* sign is a familiar sight, and although statistics show more and more Mexicans shop in American-style supermarkets, traditional markets continue to thrive in the city. *Mercados* bring the farm, the earth, and a bit of the past into everyday life. In the Palacio Nacional, Diego Rivera's panoramic mural of an Aztec Mercado, he depicts a butcher offering a human arm for sale, but in other ways the scene is as familiar to today's viewer as it was to those of old. Beans, squash, avocados, *metates* for grinding corn and *molcajetes* for grinding chilies, baskets and woven mats are just a few of the things that connect today's Mexican market to its Aztec predecessor. And, of course, the best handmade tortillas are still sold by women who sit on the ground outside with their wares in baskets, as they have for centuries. Most market stalls are small family-run businesses, so there is an intimate feel of village life in the mercado. You can still ask for *un aguacate para hoy,* a recommendation for the best melon, or get a free apple as a *pilón* (gift) from your friendly local greengrocer. Vendors beseech you with "*Qué va a llevar?*" or "*Qué le damos, marchanta?*" (What are you going to take?, What can we sell you, customer?). There is a chatty, bustling feel to the proceedings and usually, somewhere, music is playing.

Note: Markets generally close around 5-6pm

Mercado Coyoacán (see Coyoacán map)
-Chilies, moles, ceramics, baskets
This traditional market, once frequented by Frida Kahlo herself, is picturesque, attracting tourists both domestic and foreign; some craft items are sold here.

Mercado Jamaica, at Av. Congreso de la Union
and Morelos (not on map)
Metro: Jamaica, south of the Centro Histórico
- Flowers, produce
This is the main retail market for flowers and it is a must-see.
Arriving by metro, (Metro Jamaica) enter the first building
and keep walking back to the rear where you find the flowers,
mountains of them, at amazingly low prices. In the main
building are several stands serving *tepache* and *huaraches*.

Mercado Medellín, located between Medellín & Monterrey,
Coahuila & Campeche, Roma
- Seafood, moles, chilies, South American foods, Yucatecan
products
This neighborhood market in the heart of La Roma is known
for its high quality merchandise, especially seafood. The stall
across from La Morenita offers great mole pastes, chilies and
other dried spices and nuts. There are several stalls catering
to South Americans and Cubans: you can find mate or malta
here. On Saturdays only, look for the lady with a basket full of
huge banana-leaf-wrapped Colombian tamales.

Mercado Merced (Anillo de Circunvalción,
6 blocks east of the Zócalo)
Metro: Merced
- Wild mushrooms, unusual produce and prepared foods,
cookware and everything else under the sun
La Merced is huge, with several buildings housing fruits,
vegetables, chilies, meats, fish, and cookware. There is a small
section of handicrafts on the lower level, marked "*desnivel.*"
During summer months vendors from outlying regions bring
in wild mushrooms and indigenous herbs and vegetables. The
best time to go is around 10 in the morning to avoid crowds.
Arriving by metro you will be right inside when you exit from
the front of the train. Located in a dicey area, it is best not to
carry anything valuable.

Mercado San Juan Ernesto Pugibet, across from the Telmex tower, (one block below Ayuntamiento) Centro
Metro: Salto de Agua
- Imported cheeses, Asian produce, wild mushrooms, fine quality fish and meats
This market, whose history as a purveyor of imported goods dates back to the colonial era, is where professional chefs and serious cooks shop for the highest quality meat, fish, cheese, sausage, and produce in the city. **La Catalana** produces its own *embutidos* (preserved meats), and **Gastronomica San Juan** (stall no. 162) sells artisanal Spanish and Italian cheeses as well as some surprisingly good ones made here – and they are happy to let you sample before you buy. During the rainy season stand no. 261 has an incredible selection of exotic mushrooms including morels and fresh chanterelles; the dried versions are sold all year round and can be brought out of the country (I've never had any problems with customs.) Try the empanadas sold from a basket out front by a venerable Argentine gentleman, **El "Che" Burnett**. For the adventurous, there are *gusanos* (worms found in maguey cactus), which are eaten live rolled up in a tortilla, as well as armadillos and other exotic fauna.

Mercado San Juan de Los Arcos de Belén
Av. Arcos de Belen and Lopez (on the corner as you exit metro Salto de Agua)
- Moles, chiles, chorizos, traditional cheeses,
prepared foods and salsas
This is an old-fashioned market featuring traditional foods and is not to be confused with the fancier Mercado San Juan which is nearby. This is also a good market to eat in. La **Olla de Abundancia** serves great pozole.

Mercado Xochimilco (centro of Xochimilco)
- Unusual plants and prepared foods, ceramics
This old market in the heart of the southern part of the city is

as close to a country market as you will find, as many people come in from the outlying areas to sell their goods. It is particularly folkloric; look for the stand selling delicious *tamales de elote* (fresh sweet corn) and the vendors outside who sell local herbs and vegetables.

SHOPS:

CENTRO

Dulcería Celaya (1874) Cinco de Mayo 39, Centro
Monday-Friday 8:30am-6pm
Saturday 8:30am-3:30pm
- Traditional Mexican sweets
This justly famous traditional sweets shop has preserved its beautiful mid-19th century facade and interior. For sale are an array of classic Mexican sweets such as cajeta and marzipan. Try the limes filled with coconut, my favorite.

El Molinero Progreso
Calle Aranda 26, around the corner from Mercado San Juan, Centro
Open Monday-Saturday 8am-8pm
- Moles, spices, grains, chilies, nuts, flours
This store looks small but has a surprising stock; it's one of the few places that sells spices used in Indian cooking, as well as traditional Mexican ingredients.

Productos de Oaxaca Calle Santisíma 21-A, 22,
Centro (not on map)
- Mole, chocolate, special chilies, ceramics
In the depths of the Centro, this small street is home to several businesses catering to Oaxacan residents. Available are fresh Oaxacan chocolate, cheeses, and several chilies including the rare and more expensive chilhuacle. Also for sale are ceramics and other Oaxacan crafts. There are a couple of tamal vendors but otherwise no prepared food.

La Europea - branches:
Lopez 60 & Ayuntamiento 25, Centro,
Arquímedes 119, Polanco
other branches throughout the city
- Tequilas, liquors, wines
La Europea is a chain with good selections of wines and tequilas.

Café Jekemir
Isabel la Católica 72, near Mesones, Centro
- Coffee
The shop has the best coffee in the city and also the cheapest.
You can sit and have coffee and pastries (see p.107)

CONDESA / ROMA

Al Malak Productos Arabes
Av. Cuauhtémoc 160 at Guanajuato, Roma
Open daily 9:30am-7 pm
- Middle Eastern foods, ingredients
This shop and restaurant sells the best Lebanese
pastries I've ever had. Also available are olives, nuts, couscous and breads. There is also a small restaurant.

Bistro Mosaico
Michoacán near Insurgentes, Condesa
- Prepared foods, pastries, breads
This fashionable bistro has a take-out charcuterie section (see p.86)

La Naval
Corner of Michoacán & Insurgentes, Condesa
Tel.: 5584-3500
Open Monday-Saturday 10-9pm, Sunday until 5
- Wines and liquors, imported cheeses, imported products such as oils and vinegars

This is one of the best wine and liquor stores in the city, with a good bakery and deli counter as well. Trained staff can help you select from the extensive array of tequilas and wines.

Mikasa
San Luis Potosí 170 near Monterey, Roma
Tel.: 5584-3430
Open Monday-Saturday 10-7pm, Sunday until 4
- Japanese and other Asian ingredients, fresh tofu
This pan-Asian supermarket serves the Japanese community. There is excellent take-out food as well as Asian ingredients and fresh produce, seafood and tofu. You can buy lunch and walk over to nearby Parque Mexico in Condesa for a picnic, or eat at a table in front of the store. On weekends there is a lively outdoor Japanese barbeque during the day.

Orígenes Organicos
Plaza Popocatépetl 41ª, Condesa
Tel. 5208-6678, 5525-9359
- organic produce, health foods, prepared foods
A small, but well stocked shop which serves a lunch at tables overlooking the pretty plaza.

The Green Corner (3 branches)
Mazatlán No.81, Condesa
Av. Miguel.Angel de Quevedo No. 353, Coyoacán
Homero No. 1210, Polanco (not on map)
- Health food products, organic foods
These are the largest health food stores in the city with a wide range of organic products, including cosmetics.

COYOACAN / SAN ANGEL

Super Oriental
División del Norte 2515, corner Londres, Coyoacán
(not on map)
Tel: 5688-2981
Open Monday-Saturday 9:30am-7:30pm
Sunday 10:30am-3:30pm
- Asian foods and cooking supplies, kitchen utensils
This store has the city's largest selection of pan-Asian foods, sauces, dried ingredients, pastas, and cookware. It is at the end of the same street the Casa Frida Kahlo is on.

El Secreto
Av. de la Paz 58, San Angel
Tel. 5616-4511
Open Tuesday-Saturday 10-8pm, Sunday until 4
- locally made salsas, dressings, jams, take out foods and teas
A good place for gifts

Tamales Especiales, Centenario # 180, about 5 blocks from the main plaza, Coyoacán,
Tel: 5554-5996
Open   Monday-Saturday   9   am-5pm,   Friday-Sunday 6pm-9pm
- Tamales
Run by the same tamal-making family for generations, this take-out establishment has various kinds of tamales to go, and also serves tamales and atole in their garden on weekend evenings.

Trattoria della Casa Nuova
Avenida de la Paz 58-M, San Angel
- Breads and baked goods, Italian cheeses, meats, fresh pastas
(see p.90)

POLANCO

Panadería Da Silva
Oscar Wilde 12, Polanco
Tel: 5280-9875
- Breads
This Portuguese-run bakery makes the best breads in the city, hands down.

La Criolla - 2 branches:
Julio Verne, 90, Polanco
Monte Everest 760, Lomas (not on map)
-Wines, cheeses, imported "gourmet" products
These are the best gourmet stores in these areas.

Dumas Gourmet
Alejandro Dumas 125, near Mazaryk, Polanco
Tel.: 5280-1925/8385
Open Monday - Friday 8am - 8pm, Saturday 10am - 9pm, Sunday 11am - 6pm
- Chef Sonia El-Nawal, an ex-New Yorker of Lebanese descent, has opened a sleek "traiteur" style store with interesting Mediterranen dishes to eat at home as well as good breads and gourmet products.

Adonis
Homero 424, Polanco
Open daily 9:30am -7pm
Tel. 5250-2064
Branch : Av. Universidad 644, col. Del Valle
Tel. 5604-9457
- Middle Eastern foods, ingredients
This large shop sells good middle-eastern pastries, fresh cheeses, olives, nuts, packaged foods and breads. There is a good restaurant around the corner.

Also see:
La Europea, The Green Corner, above

LOMAS

Eno
Explanada 730, Lomas de Chapultepec (not on map)
- Gourmet take-out, sandwiches
Chef Enrique Olvera of Pujol has opened this shop and the bread is from Da Silva; how can they go wrong...

Centro Gourmet Vittorio (not on map)
Prolongación Bosques de Reforma 1371
Bosques de las Lomas
Tel. 5251 3186 / 5596 9257
-fresh pasta and Italian products

Also see:
La Criolla, above

GLOSSARY

GLOSSARY

A

aceite de oliva – olive oil

aceituna – olive

acelgas – Swiss chard

achiote – a mild aromatic red paste made of seeds of the same name often used in Yucatecan cooking

agri-dulce - sweet & sour

aguas frescas -   (or **aguas preparadas**) literally "fresh waters," these are traditional drinks made with fresh fruits or vegetables pureed in a blender with sugar and water. They are found in most Mexican restaurants and food stalls, although sometimes you won't see them on the menu, so be sure to ask. The most common flavors are jamaica (hibiscus flower), tamarindo (pulp from tamarind seeds) and horchata (made from rice or sometimes almonds; there is no milk in this white drink). Popular fruits include mango, papaya, watermelon, and cantaloupe. Plain purified drinking water is called **agua natural**, bubbly water **agua mineral**, bottled water **agua embotellada**, a simple glass of water *"un vaso con agua."*

ahumado – smoked

al pastor - see pastor

albahaca – basil

alcaparras – capers

alga – seaweed

almeja – clam

almendra – almond

almuerzo – light lunch, brunch

alubias – white beans

amargo/a – bitter

anafre - a charcoal brazier

anchoa – anchovy

ancas de rana – frogs legs

añejo – aged (when referring to tequila or cheese)

anguila – eel

ante - an old fashioned layered dessert

antojitos -   refers to a food category, not a dish, but you will see the word often. Its meaning (literally "before the eyes") can vary, but it usually refers to corn-based appetizers, anything made with tortillas or *masa de maíz* (corn dough.) They are eaten as a light meal or snack (although they can often be quite filling). Some of the most common antojitos found in Mexico City are quesadillas, tlacoyos, gorditas, sopes, panuchos, tacos, tamales, huaraches, and enchiladas.

apio – celery

arenque – herring

asado – roasted

ate - a paste made of dried fruit, usually eaten as dessert with cheese

atole – a drink thickened with maize and flavored with fruit or vanilla or coffee and usually served in the morning or evening with tamales. The chocolate version is called **champurrado**

atún – tuna fish ("*tuna*" is a cactus fruit)

avena – oatmeal

aves – poultry

B

bacalao – salt cod (bacalao fresco is fresh cod but is rarely seen in Mexico)

barbacoa – usually sheep or goat, baked in a pit in maguey leaves, served as tacos. Common in central Mexico as a fiesta or wedding dish.

berenjena – eggplant

berros - watercress

betabel – beet (known as **remolacha** en Spain)

birria – a spicy stew usually made with goat or mutton, often served during festive periods such as Christmas, New Year's Eve and at weddings. Originally from Jalisco, but now widespread in central Mexico, it is served with tortillas, onion, cilantro, lime, salsa and typically, with a bowl of its own broth as accompaniment.

bolillo – a crusty roll, common throughout Mexico

botanas – hors d'oevres

brocheta – brochette (shish kabob)

burrito – wheat flour tortilla roll, rarely found in central Mexico, more of a Tex-Mex creation.

budín – literally pudding, often a savory

budín azteca is like lasagna made with tortillas and salsa verde.

C

cabrito – kid, baby goat

cabeza – head

cabra – goat (**queso de cabra** is goat cheese)

cacahuate- peanut (known as "maní" in most of the Spanish speaking world outside of Mexico)

calabaza – winter squash

calabacita – summer squash, like zucchini

calamares – squid

caldo – broth

camarones – shrimp ("gambas" in Spain)

camote – sweet potato; *camoteros,* (sweet potato vendors) circulate in the evenings, their carts emitting a whistle like an old steam engine, which announces their presence. Camotes are served with brown sugar syrup or condensed milk.

canela – cinnamon

cangrejo – crab (also called *jaiba*)

capiroteada - a bread pudding made with brown sugar

castaña – chestnut

cebolla – onion

cerdo –pork (also **puerco**)

cereza – cherry

cerveza – beer (*oscura* is dark, *clara*, light)

ceviche – seafood that has been "cooked" by marinating in citrus juice; there are many regional variations, but the best is found on the Pacific coast

chilpachole - a hearty soup from the Veracruz region featuring crabs and chile broth

champiñones – mushrooms (sometimes called *hongos*)

chamorro – a big roasted hunk of pork leg.

chapulines – grasshoppers, eaten deep fried

chayote – a green squash-like vegetable

chela - slang for a beer

chícharros- peas

chicharrón – porkskin, eaten deep fried or in stews

chilaquiles – crisp tortillas chips sauted in salsa – a typical breakfast dish, often served with eggs or chicken.

chiles en nogada – green poblano chilies filled with a mixture of ground meat and raisins or other dried fruit, topped with a white sauce made of ground pecans and cream and sprinkled with pomegranate seeds. It is usually served at room temperature. The three colors represent the Mexican flag. This classic dish from Puebla is popular around Fiestas Patrias (Independence Day) in September, but is served year-round in some restaurants.

chilpachole – a crab soup with a chili broth, from Veracruz

chongos zamoranos – traditional curdled milk dessert

chorizo – sausage; there are many varieties including a mysteriously bright green one from Toluca.

chuleta – chop, usually pork

churros – a Spanish dessert, fried dough pressed through a mold

ciruela (pasa) – plum (prune)

clemole - a liquidy, soupy type of mole

cochinita pibil – Yucatecan shredded pork, cooked with chilies and spices

comida – lunch. This is the main meal of the day for most Mexicans; it is usually not eaten before 2pm and often lasts for hours. Many nicer restaurants don't even open their doors until 1:30pm, but people will really start to arrive at 2:30-3pm. Mexicans love to *sobremesar*, or sit around and chat after eating. The American idea of eating, paying and leaving seems strange to Mexicans, and it is considered rude to be handed the check without asking for it.

comida corrida – a complete meal consisting of soup, rice, main course, often dessert and beverage which can be had for a few dollars. You will see these words in fondas and *comedores*, simple eateries that cater to working class Mexicans looking for an economic home-cooked meal. Sometimes the food is bland and watery, but you can also find hearty and delicious meals.

cena – dinner. In most Mexican homes the evening meal is usually a simple affair, such as a soup or tamales, but "going out for dinner," is becoming more a part of Mexico City nightlife. Cena is normally served after 9pm.

coca - the popular name for Coca Cola

coco - coconut

codos - elbow macaroni (literally "elbows")

cogollos - lettuce hearts, a term from Spain occasionally seen on Mexican menus

comal - a metal or ceramic plate on which tortillas are cooked

cordoníz – quail

col – cabbage (also known as repollo)

colado – strained (as for orange juice)

coliflor – cauliflower

conejo – rabbit

costillas – ribs

Cuba - a rum and Coke

cuitlacoche (also spelled **huitlacoche**) – black corn fungus with a subtle mushroom taste

D

derecho - straight up, as for drinks

dulces – sweets, candy

durazno – peach

E

elote – fresh corn (not usually sweet)

enchiladas – literally means "chilied" – tortillas in a variety of sauces, filled or not.
endibia – endive
ensalada – salad (**ensalada mixta** is made of cooked vegetables, **ensalada verde** is a green salad)
entremeses – appetizers
epazote – a medicinal-tasting herb used in many dishes, especially black beans and quesadillas
espinacas – spinach; many leafy greens carry this label
espuma – foam
esquites – fresh corn with onion and chillies, sometimes served with sour cream or mayonaise; a street food
estofado – stew

F

filete – fillet, usually means beef, unless in the context of a fish dish
flautas - an antojito, rolled, deep fried long tortillas containing chicken, meat or potato, served with green salsa, cream and lettuce
flor – flower (**flor de calabaza** – squash blossom flower)
frambuesa – raspberry
fresa – strawberry
fideos – noodles
frijoles –beans; *charros*, beans in broth with meats, chorizos and chilies, *refritos*, mashed and sauteed.
frito – fried
frutas secas – dried fruits

G

galleta – cookie or cracker
gallina – hen
gambas – large shrimp
gelatina – gelatine or Jello

gengibre - ginger

ginebra – gin

gorditas -   pockets of corn masa cooked on a griddle and stuffed with beans, meat, nopales; one of the most common street foods in Mexico City

granada – pomegranate; **granada china** is a passion fruit

grasa, grasosa – grease, greasy

grosella - currant

guiso, guisado – any cooked or prepared dish, such as a stew or mole

gusano –worm

H

haba – fava bean

harina –flour

helado – ice cream

hervido – boiled

hielo – ice

hierbabuena - mint

hígado – liver

higo – fig

hinojo – fennel

hoja – leaf (**hoja santa** or hierba santa is an aromatic leaf used in Oaxacan cooking)

hongos - mushrooms

horchata – (pronounced "orCHATa") a sweet drink usually made from rice; often one of the *aguas frescas* choices in a restaurant

horno, horneado – oven, baked

huachinango – red snapper

huarache – a large thick tortilla topped with meat or cheese; so-called because it is the size and shape of a shoe

huauzontles – a green vegetable resembling unripe goldenrod, usually made into a patty and served in tomato broth. You have to pull the stems out as you eat like you do when eating an artichoke.

hueso – bone

huevos – eggs

    revueltos – scrambled

    a la Mexicana – scrambled with chopped tomato, chile, onion

    rancheros – fried with red salsa

    motuleños – layered tortilla, black bean, ham, fresh cheese, fried egg and salsa

    albañiles – scrambled with dark chile salsa

    estrellados – sunny side up

huitlacoche - see cuitlacoche

J

jabalí – wild boar

jaiba – crab

jamón – ham

jarra - pitcher, such as for drinks

jengibre – ginger

jícama – a slightly sweet white root vegetable, eaten raw

jitomate – tomato (also called tomate)

judía – white bean

jugo - juice

L

langosta – lobster

leña – firewood "**a la leña**"- cooked over wood fire

lengua – tongue

lenguado – sole (fish)

lentejas – lentils

liebre – wild hare

lima – sweet limes used in Yucatecan cuisine

limón – green lime (yellow lemons are rare in Mexico)

lomo – loin, usualy of pork

M

machaca – dried beef, typical of the north

maguey – agave cactus used to make pulque, tequila and mezcal

maíz – corn

manchamanteles - literally "tablecloth stainers" a pork dish with chile sauce and fruit

manteca – lard

mantequilla – butter

manzana – apple

mariscos – seafood, shellfish

masa – dough

médula – bone marrow

mejillón – mussel

melón – cantaloupe melon

membrillo – quince

menta – peppermint

menudo – tripe stew, popular as a hangover remedy

merienda – afternoon snack, like English tea

metate - stone implement for grinding corn

merluza – hake, a firm white fish

mezcal - a variation of tequila, made from agave as well as other cactus plants. Mainly produced in the state of Oaxaca, the quality ranges from rotgut to fine and aged. It has a smoky, almost charcoal-like taste. A worm is often included in each bottle, for flavor, luck or both.

miel – honey

migajas – crumbs

milanesa – breaded and fried beef or chicken

mixiotes – a cooking style in which meat, often mutton, together with spices and chilies, is wrapped in a leaf or parchment paper and cooked

mojarra – perch, a fish often served whole and deep fried

molcajete – traditional mortar made of volcanic stone

mole – a sauce containing many ingredients such as herbs, chillies, vegetables, and thickened with seeds such as pepita, sesame or peanut. Some dark moles contain a small amount of chocolate, but calling mole a "chocolate sauce" is erroneous. Mole also refers to the dish. The most famous mole, Poblano, was supposedly invented in the convent of Santa Clara in Puebla, but most likely developed as a blending of indigenous and European techniques and ingredients. Oaxaca is known for its seven moles. Mole is considered by many to be the national dish of Mexico, hence the expression "Más Mexicano que mole", or "As Mexican as mole."

molletes – a breakfast dish of bolillos, or rolls, spread with refried beans and topped with melted cheese.

morcilla – blood sausage (also called morongo)

mostaza – mustard

N

nabo – turnip

nachos - an American concoction of tortilla chips and melted cheese rarely seen in Mexico

naranja – orange

naranja agria – sour (Seville) orange

nieve – sorbet (literally "snow")

nopales - cactus paddles eaten as a vegetable throughout Mexico available at most taco and tlacoyo stands. **Ensalada de nopalitos** (cactus salad with onions, cilantro, and tomato), which you will find on many menus, is a good way to try them. Nopales have a mild, slightly acidic, green bean-like flavor and, if not cooked properly, emit a slimy liquid like okra.

nuez – pecan-like nut

nuez de Castilla - walnuts

nuez moscada – nutmeg

P

paleta – ice pop, usually made of fruit

palillo – toothpick

palomitas – popcorn

pambazo - a soft roll sandwich stuffed and deep fried

pan – bread

pan árabe – Arab bread, or pita

pan dulce – sweet bread or rolls

panuchos – a Yucatecan dish consisting of a fried tortilla, spread with black bean paste, *cochinita pibil* (pork) and salsa

papa – potato (called **patata** in Spain)

papas a la Francesa – French fries

papadzules – a Yucatecan dish, meatless, of tortillas, crumbled boiled egg, and a pumpkin seed sauce

parillada – mixed grill

pasa – raisin

pastel – cake

pastor – **tacos al pastor**, a dish of Arab influence, which appeared only in the 1960's. Meat is roasted on a revolving skewer, shaved off and served as an open taco, often with pineapple, and a selection of salsas. A specialty of Mexico City

pata – foot (literally "paw")

pato – duck

pavo – turkey (also known as *guajolote*)

pay - pie

pechuga – breast (of chicken, usually), does not refer to humans

pepinillo – pickle

pepino – cucumber

pera – pear

perejíl – parsley

pescado – fish (as food; the animal is called *pez*)

pez espada - swordfish

picadillo – chopped meat with tomatoes and chile, often with rainis or nuts, used as filling for chilies or tacos

picante – hot, spicy (*caliente* refers to temperature)

pierna – leg (of pork or lamb when refering to food)

piloncillo – dark brown sugar, usually sold in the shape of a cone

pimentón – green or sweet red pepper

pimienta – black pepper

piña – pineapple

piñon – pine nut, pignole

pipián – a sauce and a dish, green or red, similar to mole, but simpler, based on pumpkin seeds (*pepitas*) as a thickener.

plátano – banana

plátano macho – plantain

poblano – the large chile used for rellenos (literally someone or something from Puebla)

poc chuc – Yucatecan pork chop, grilled and served with sour orange sauce

pollo – chicken

popote – drinking straw

postre –dessert

pozole - a thick satisfying soup, almost a stew. Red pozole, the most common, has a pork and tomato base, contains large corn kernels (hominy), and is served with radish, lettuce, onion and oregano, which you add according to taste.

puchero – hearty meat soup or stew

porro – leek

puerco - pork, pig

pulque - A drink made by fermenting sap of the maguey cactus. It has a thick texture and a yeasty taste. **Curados** are pulques that have been flavored with fruits, vegetables or nuts. Pulque was used in Aztec rituals and has a long association as a drink of the common man. It is usually served only in **pulquerias** which had been slowly disappearing, but seem to be making a comeback as fashionable places for young people to meet.

Q

quesadillas -most commonly, a large corn tortilla filled, folded and cooked on a round metal griddle, or sometimes deep-fried. There are many kinds of fillings, common are flor de calabaza (cheese and squash blossom flowers), huitlacoche (a corn fungus with a mushroom-like taste), and quelites (a spinach-like green).

queso – cheese

queso añejo – aged cheese

queso azul – blue cheese

queso crema – cream cheese (also known as "queso Filadelfia" for obvious reasons)

queso de cabra – goat's milk cheese

queso de soja (or soya) – tofu

queso fresco – fresh mild white cheese

queso fundido – cheese melted in a casserole, sometimes with chorizo, in which case
it is a *choriqueso*

queso manchego- not the good Spanish stuff, but a bland aged white cheese

queso oaxaqueño – stringy cheese that comes rolled up and melts nicely.

queso ranchero – slightly aged cow's milk cheese

queso requesón – crumbly and creamy, like farmer or dry cottage cheese

R

rábano – radish

rabo – tail (as in oxtail)

rebanada – slice, usually of cake

rana - frog

recado – a marinade or paste for meat, from the Yucatan

refresco – soda pop

repollo - cabbage (a word used more in Spain)

res - beef

riñón – kidney

robalo – sea bass

romero – rosemary

ron – rum

S

sal – salt

salchicha – hot dog

salsa – sauce

inglesa – Worchester

mexicana - fresh tomato, onion, chile, cilantro & lime

soya – soy sauce

picante – hot sauce

verde – green, made with *tomates verdes* and chile

roja – red, made with tomato or just chiles

sandía – watermelon

sálvia – sage

sangrita –a drink made with tomato and orange or pomegranate juice, lime, and spices, and almost always served with straight tequila as a chaser

semilla – seed

sémola – semolina

sesos – brains

sopa - soup. Consomé de pollo or caldo de pollo is chicken soup usually with lots of chicken and vegetables. Other common soups are sopa de tortilla or sopa azteca, made with chicken broth, tomatoes, chilies, crisp tortilla strips, avocado and cheese. Sopa de flor de calabaza, made with squash blossoms, and sopa de ajo, garlic soup are also traditional favorites.

sopes - small discs of corn masa fried and then topped with beans, chicken, chorizo, the variety is endless These are often served as appetizers in restaurants or at stalls.

T

tacos - The crispy shells filled with ground beef, cheddar cheese and lettuce that are sold as tacos in the U.S. are not found in Mexico. A taco here is a soft corn tortilla with a small amount of filling, rolled up and eaten with your hands. Tacos are found everywhere, eaten day and night, and are considered essential to most Mexican diets. Meat is the preferred filling, but vegetable and seafood can also be found. Most popular are **carnitas** (chopped roast pork), **barbacoa** (pit-cooked sheep or goat), **chicharrón** (pork rind), but you can also find tacos made with eyes, ears, nose and brain. **Tacos al pastor** reflect Arab influence in Mexican cuisine: small slices of seasoned pork are cut from a rotating spindle and served with a bit of pineapple, chopped onion and cilantro.

A good *taquería* will have an alluring selection of salsas to spice things up. Another type of taco is **tacos de guisado**, stuffed with cooked or stewed fillings, often with vegetables.

tamales -Tamales (the singular is "tamal") vary from region to region and are found all over Latin America, often with different names. Basically a tamal is ground corn wrapped in a husk (usually corn but sometimes a banana leaf) and steamed for hours. The masa (corn dough) is mixed with lard and usually contains a small amount of filling: chicken or pork with red sauce, green sauce, or mole; and strips of chile poblano with cheese are the most common. Tamales Oaxaqueños are wrapped in banana leaves and have a smoother, denser texture. The filling is really only a flavoring—the main event is the corn itself, its flavor and texture. To eat a tamal, you discard the corn husk or banana leaf. Tamales are usually eaten in the morning and at night. In residential neighborhoods, market areas, outside metro stations, and around the Zócalo, street corner vendors tend shiny steel containers with steam escaping from the edges. Because tamales cook for many hours and are sold hot, they are a dependably hygienic street food.

taquería- an establishment serving tacos

taza – cup, for coffee or tea

té – tea
 - *de manzanilla* – camomile
 - *negro* – black tea
 - *de menta* or *hierbabuena* - mint
 - *de limón* – lemongrass, generally only used as a medicnal

Tequila -   Mexico's most famous alcohol is distilled from the sap of the agave cactus. Many foreigners only drink it mixed as margaritas, but few Mexicans order it that way. If you want to drink like a native, order "*un tequila*" (not "*una*" *tequila*) with **sangrita** (literally "little blood"). You will be served two small glasses, one with straight tequila and one with a spicy red drink made of tomato juice with various additions, usually pomegranate or orange juice and hot sauce. Alternate sips from the two glasses. There are three basic types of tequila: **blanco, reposado,** and **añejo**. Reposados are aged, usually amber colored and are more expensive; blancos are clear and have a stronger bite; and añejos have been aged longer and tend to be smoother. Most bars have good selections, which waiters can explain, but be sure to check prices since some can be very expensive.

ternera – veal, usually not as young as the American or Italian variety

tlayuda – a large type of quesadilla, native to Oaxaca

tlacoyos - a common *antojito*, satisfying and delicious, found on street corners and near markets throughout the city. Almost always made by women sitting on the ground with a *comal* (a charcoal burner with a round metal or clay plate on top), this wonderful food was probably eaten by the Aztecs in much the same form. Blue or yellow corn *masa* (dough) is formed by hand into a small lozenge, flattened, and filled with *requesón* (fresh cheese), *habas* (fava beans) or *frijoles* then cooked on a dry griddle and topped with chopped nopales (cactus), onions, cilantro, grated cheese and your choice of red or green salsa. Tlacoyos, considered common street food, are rarely found in restaurants.

tocino – bacon

tomate verde - sometimes known as **tomatillo**, this is not a green tomato, but an entirely different fruit

toronja –grapefruit

tortas - Mexico´s version of the sandwich,

supposedly invented by an Italian immigrant at the turn of the 20th century, is a *bolillo* (soft roll) with a wide range of ingredients. A few popular choices are *milanesa* (breaded and fried meat), *pierna* (roast pork), and *choriqueso* (cheese and sausage), but the variety is endless. Garnishes include tomato, onion, avocado, cheese, lettuce, mayonnaise, and of course, chile jalapeño or chipotle.

tortillas- the staff of life of Mexican cuisine, and the only true pre-Hispanic food, the ubiquitous tortilla is essentially ground corn, softened with cal or limestone, called *nixtamal*, flattened into a 6-inch disc and cooked on a dry griddle. (Tortillas made of wheat are more common in the north.) Millions of tortillas are eaten daily—and have been for centuries. They are the basic ingredient for tacos, enchiladas, tostadas, burritos, chilaquiles, flautas and a host of other Mexican dishes.

tostada – a tortilla fried crisp and topped with various ingredients

totopos – fried tortilla chips

trigo – wheat

tripas - tripe

trucha – trout

tuna – prickly pear (cactus) fruit, NOT the fish, which is *atún*

tuétano – marrow

turrón – nougat, like the Italian candy

U

ultramarinos - an old-fashioned word meaning delicatessan-type foods, such as sausage, cheese etc.

uvas – grapes

uva pasa – raisin

V

vaca – cow (the animal - the meat is *res*)

venado – deer, venison

Veracruzana – from Veracruz, in cooking generally refers to a tomato, chile, caper, olive sauce.

vapor – steam: *al vapor* is steamed

verduras – vegetables

vinagre – vinegar

vino – wine

  vino tinto – red

  vino blanco – white

  rosado –rosé

  de Jerez – Sherry

  seco – dry

  espumoso - bubbly

vuelve a la vida – literally "return to life", a seafood cocktail containing everything in the ocean

Z

zanahoria – carrot

zapote – *zapote negro* is a black tropical fruit, usually served prepared with orange juice and liqour and eaten as a dessert.

zarzamora – blackberry

zarzuela – literally a "mixture" or "hodgepodge", sometimes seen as "*zarzuela de mariscos*" a seafood casserole. The word also refers to Spanish light opera.

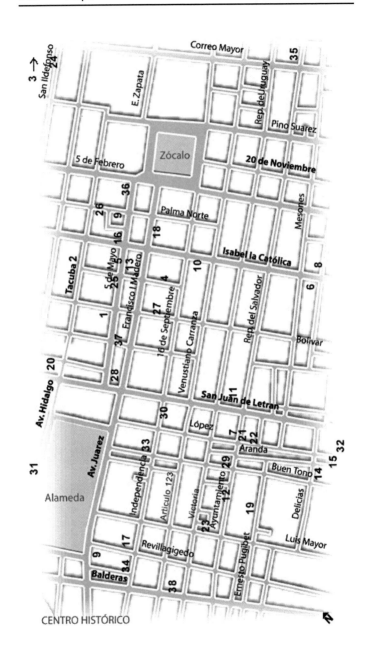

CENTRO HISTÓRICO

EL CENTRO HISTORICO

1 Bar La Opera - p.108
2 Cafe Tacuba - p.55
3 Carnitas Michoacanas "Don One" - p.32
4 Casa del Pavo La - p.41
5 Café la Blanca - p.41
6 Coox Hanal - p.56
7 Caguamo El - p.23
8 Café Jekemir - p.105
9 Cardenal El - p.75
10 Casino Español - p.82
11 Churrería el Moro - p.102
12 El Paisa - p.43
13 Dulcería Celaya - p.121
14 Fonda Mi Lupita - p.42
15 Gran Cocina Mi Fonda La - p.42
16 Gilipollos, Jugos Canadá - p.34, p.37
17 Lincoln Restaurante - p.57
18 Marisqueria Palmas - p.43
19 Mercado San Juan - p.26
20 Mesón Andaluz El - p.85
21 Mi Taco Yucateco - p.30
22 Molinero El - p.121
23 Tortas El Cuadrilatero - p.45
24 Pozole Doña Yoli - p.26
25 Puerta del Sol La - p.109
26 Cantina La Montañosa - p.109
27 Salón Corona - p.111
28 Sanborn's - p.57
29 Taqueria "El Huequito" - p.43
30 Taquería Tlaquepaque - p.44
31 Tlacoyo stand Franz Mayor Museum – p.28
32 Mercado San Juan Arcos de Belen -p.120
33 Tio Pepe El - p.109
34 Texcocana La - p.45
35 Tortas Been - p.35
37 Zinco Jazz Club - p.110
38 Jugos Balderas - p.37

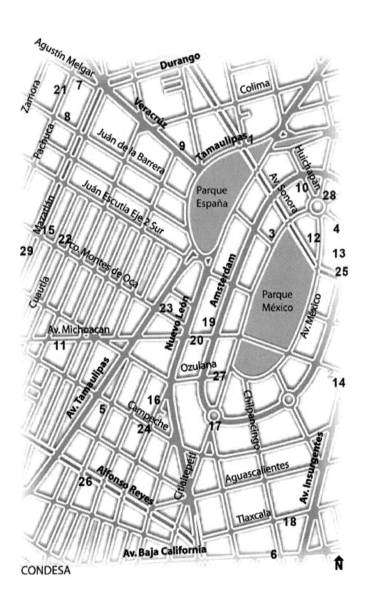

CONDESA

LA CONDESA

1 La Balance Pâtisserie -p.105
2 Bistro Mosaico – p.84
3 Bistro Rojo – p.84
4 La Bodega – p.59
5 La Botica Mezcalería – p.112
6 Caldos de Gallina/Flautas Chilpancingo - p.22
7 Casa D'Italia – p.86
8 Chocolatería Mamá Sarita – p.102
9 Condesa DF – p.111
10 Flor De Lis – p.61
11 Gelatería Neve & Gelato –p.104
12 Hip Kitchen – p.76
13 El Jamil – p.86
14 La Naval – p.123
15 Neveria Roxy – p.104
16 La Ostra – p.61
17 Photo Bistro – p.87
18 Tacos de Guisados Tlaxcala – p.22
19 Taquería "El Guero".- p.47
20 Taquería "El Greco" – p.46
21 Tianguis Condesa (Tuesday) – p. 23
22 Tio Luis – p.62
23 El Tizoncito – p.60
24 Tianguis (Friday) – p.25
25 Jugos Sonora – p.37
26 Agapi Mu – p.84
27 Maque – p.105
28 Origenes Organicos – p.123
29 The Green Corner – p.123

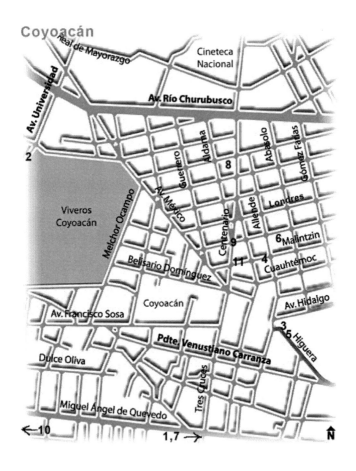

COYOACAN

1 La Bella Lula - p.65
2 Las Chupacabras – p.30
3 La Guadalupana – p.113
4 El Morral – p.63
5 Mercado de Antojitos – p.28
6 Mercado Coyoacán – p.36
7 El Tajín – p.76
8 Tamales Especiales – p.124
9 La Parroquia – p.103
10 La Lechuza – p.31
11 La Barraca Valenciana – p.36

POLANCO

1 Solea – p.78
2 Alto Tango – p.103
3 Área del Hotel Hábita – p.114
4 El Bajío – p.74
5 Bellaria – p.89
6 Benkay – p.90
7 Blue Lounge – p.114
8 Le Cirque – p.92
9 Izote – p.77
10 O'Mei – p.94
11 Los Panchos – p.64
12 Pujol – p.77
13 Adonis – p.125
14 El Rey del Taco – p.33
15 Panadería Da Silva – p.125
16 MP Bistro – p.79
17 Biko – p.90
18 Casa Portuguesa – p.91
19 D.O. – p.92
20 Jaso – p.93
21 La Europea – p.122
22 La Criolla – p.125
23 Dumas – p.125

Roma

Av. Chapultapec

Puebla

Morelia

5

Córdoba

8

Oaxaca

Durango

15

13
Jardín
Pushkia

12

Colima

3 Plaza
La Madrid

Roma
Norte

4

Olizaba

6

Medellín

Tabasco

Alvaro Obregón

16

2 Chihuahua

Av. Cuauhtemoc

14

Monterrey

Guanajuato

Mérida

11

1

Tonalá

Queretaro

San Luís Potosí

Av. Insurgentes Sur

17

Av. Yucatán

Chiapas

Coahuila

Roma Norte

Tapachula

Antonio M. Anza

7

León de los Aldama

9,10

Campeche

Nayarit

Plaza
Pabellón
Cuahutemoc

N

COLONIA ROMA

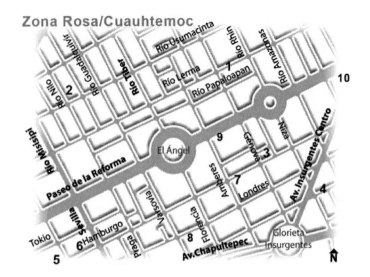

ZONA ROSA / CUAUHTEMOC

1 La Bella Lula – p.65
2 Bistrot Arlequín – p.95
3 El Dragón – p.96
4 Fonda el Refugio – p.66
6 La Texcocana – p.45
7 Tezka – p.97
8 Beatricita – p.48
9 Bistro Mosaico – p.84
10 El Bajio – p.74

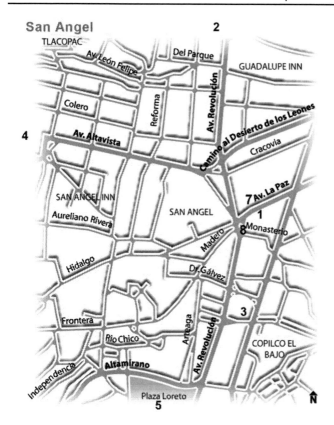

SAN ANGEL

1 Bistro Mosaico, Paxia – p.84,80
2 Fiesole – p.88
3 Mercado San Angel
4 San Angel Inn – p.113
5 Taberna del León – p.79
6 Trattoria della Casa Nuova – p.89
7 El Secreto – p.124
8 Churrería El Convento – p.103

INDEX

INDEX BY LOCATION

INDEX BY REGIONAL CUISINE

INDEX BY NATIONALITY

USEFUL WEBSITES

www.mexicocityfood.net - Updates and new information for this book

www.egullet.org - For serious gastronomes

www.chow.com - Similar to above, especially for those in search of "authentic" cuisine

www.mexicosoulandessence.com - Custom Mexico City tours with an emphasis on cuisine

www.mexonline.com - An all-around site for information about Mexico City

www.mexconnect.com - This site has a useful calendar of fairs and fiestas around Mexico

www.ticketmaster.com.mx - Offers tickets to cultural events, this is also a good place to check out what's happening in the city

www.insidemex.com - The online version of a smart, English language monthly.

http://mexicocooks.typepad.com - Info on Mexico's culinary scene.

http://mexicocitydf.blogspot.com - a blog about the city

We highly recommend the guide book:

MEXICO CITY: AN OPINIONATED GUIDE FOR THE CURIOUS TRAVELER,

by Jim Johnston and published by iUniverse, available at all major online booksellers.

"This is the guidebook I want. Wonderfully written, airtight information, organized in the smartest possible way. I can't imagine a better Mexico City guide for these times."
- Tony Cohan, author of Mexican Days and
  On Mexican Time.

"Evokes the colors, sounds and smells of the world's second-largest metropolitan area."
- San Francisco Chronicle

"This is the only guidebook to Mexico City I know that has the idiosyncratic sensibility of someone who not only lives here, but loves it and has dedicated a great deal of time, energy and consideration to his meandering. The photos are also quite evocative."

-David Lida, author of First Stop in the New World: Mexic City, the Capital of the 21st Century

ABOUT THE AUTHOR

Nicholas Gilman was born in New York City to painter Esther Gilman and theatre critic Richard Gilman. Traveling to Mexico City to study the mural movement he became interested in the traditions of Mexican painting and culture. He worked as an assistant curator at the Hispanic Society of America for several years and in 1986 won a scholarship to The New York Academy of Art to study classical painting and sculpture.

A painter and teacher, he has shown his work extensively in the USA and Mexico. He has studied gastronomy at UNAM (the National Autonomous University of Mexico), cooking at the Universidad del Claustro de Sor Juana, is a founding member of a Mexican chapter of Slow Food International, as well as member of IACP (International Association of Culinary Professionals). He was editor and photographer for the book "Mexico City: An Opinionated Guide for the Curious Traveler". He became a Mexican citizen in 2005 and lives and works in Mexico City.

www.mexicocityfood.net

4840449

Made in the USA
Lexington, KY
06 March 2010